AMERICANS
IN THEIR OWN WORDS

Nicholas Wolf
Editor

Honey Locust Press

AMERICANS IN THEIR OWN WORDS

Copyright ©2013 Nicholas Wolf
All Rights Reserved

Library of Congress Control Number: 2013941976

ISBN-13 978-1-60364-045-9
ISBN-10 1-60364-045-2

This book may not be reproduced in whole or in part, by mimeograph, photocopy, or any other means, electronic or physical, without express written permission of the copyright holder.

For information, contact:
info@honeylocustpress.com
or
Honey Locust Press
238 Park Drive NE
Ranger, GA 30734

To

the memory of my uncle

Brigadier General Alfred Wolf

forever associated with the years

when I began to dream of adventure

Preface

The Americans Steve Jobs and Bill Gates are reason enough for this book. All they ever wanted to do was change the world. Those individuals who today make this country what it is, who embody the American spirit, are a select few who change the way people lead their lives. If they come from humble beginnings, and struggle along the way, they become a part of our folklore. And if they have a positive impact on generations to come, then we call them visionaries or creative geniuses.

This book is about Americans who often go unnoticed and unnamed, who fly under the radar. As you read their personal stories, you realize they embody the same spirit that fills the select few. Contrary to that smooth upward curve we wish for in our children, there are many paths, not all of them positive, that make life's struggle exciting and worth reading about. Contributions to that spirit are related in these pages by the participants themselves.

The following excerpt from the first "commercial" transatlantic flight is a case in point if you have ever flown from New York to the UK and Europe:

...left Port Washington (New York) 9:30am, arrived Shediac 1:30pm, left Shediac 2:15pm, arrived Botwood 5:15pm, left Botwood 7:15pm, sighted land 8:20am, landed Foynes 8:30am, left Foynes 10:15pm, arrived Southampton (England) 1:45pm. Total elapsed time 28 hours 15 minutes. Total flying time 23 hours 45 minutes.

Hundreds of Americans are responsible for what seems

normal today, a flying time to England of between five and seven hours depending on weather conditions and aircraft. The people who appear in these pages descend from that group. Their stories are not rags to riches, but rather, day to day life experiences: some wishful yarn spinning, often swimming against the tide, perhaps completing a difficult journey.

The connection between the many and the genius is clear. Steve Jobs depended on engineers, programmers, teachers, factory workers, artists, truck drivers, musicians, publishers, investors, advertising executives, and not to be forgotten, the kids who staff the Genius Bars in Apple stores. Somewhere in the past there is a genius behind all of us, lest we forget. The people in these pages have not forgotten. They are on the right side of history. They are Americans.

Introduction

Not long ago a letter was discovered from General Alfred Wolf to his mother, describing the experience of flying the Atlantic as the first bona fide commercial passenger. It was bookmarked in a copy of his book: Captain Cook's Cannon, a posthumous volume describing a successful Great Barrier Reef Expedition to find the iron cannon jettisoned by His Majesty's Bark Endeavour 200 years before. General Wolf led that expedition; his wife discovered the manuscript after his death in 1985 and had it published, although few people have read it beyond members of his family.

Alfred Wolf was my father's brother, my uncle. He was described as a "well-known sportsman, pilot, and attorney" in an article in the April 19, 1938 Philadelphia Evening Public Ledger, which was reporting on the establishment on the Schuylkill River of a seaplane harbor, where he landed his pontoon equipped plane; he established the port to commute to his law firm and it is unclear if anyone else used the facility or how long it was there. Excerpts from his Pilot's Log are contained in the Appendix to this book.

A graduate of Princeton and Oxford (where he received his law degree), Wolf was charged with overseeing delivery of aircraft from factory to the Pacific War Zone Combat Command during the Second World War. In three years his command delivered 6000 aircraft throughout the Pacific War Zone with a loss rate of less than 1%. He became a Brigadier General later in life after he was re-activated during the Korean War to run the Air Force base in Wiesbaden, Germany; he moved on to become Vice Commander, first of Andrews Air Force Base and then McGuire Air Force Base. He was an advisor to the ICAO in Paris and was on the Air

Coordinating Committee for West Germany. Perhaps most important, he was a founder of the AOPA (Aircraft Owners and Pilots Association), the largest civil aviation association in the world.

He was, of course, an avid deep sea diver and pilot; his Flight Log in the Appendix will convince the reader of what he once said to his nephew: "…then comes the most difficult thing. Try to find out what you want to do. If you, at any time, are lucky enough to discover this, do it. It is the failure to indulge your every whim that makes for less than total happiness. There you have it in a nutshell."

This book is dedicated to Alfred Wolf, without question the inspiration for what has become an exciting record, in their own words, of Americans whose stories are worth the telling. Often, a recollected moment comes out that has brought the editor to tears, when he has read what was previously recorded. Or, it may be too painful, and the subject has requested deletion.

What a privilege to witness the struggles, setbacks, and triumphs of others, as each of us tries to find our way in this increasingly complicated 21st century. Sitting with the subjects of this book and hearing them pour out their stories, I am sad to recollect how we miss this intimacy most of the time. We stare at a computer screen, where most of us function today, instead of probing, in an acceptable way, the mysteries of lives that are not our own, face to face.

Nicholas Wolf

Table of Contents

Gerry Millet... 1

Mary Putnam Post Chatfield.................................. 39

Douglas Vincent O'Dell, Junior 60

Eleanor Sokoloff.. 102

Barney Berlinger... 126

Andrea Jenson... 149

Jon Hlafter... 181

Terri Gregg... 192

Taylor Allen 207

Luis Lopez... 220

Appendix (Alfred Wolf) 241

Gerry Millet

Athlete, artist, photographer, advertising executive, gallery owner

My ancestor Thomas Millet, an indentured servant, came to Dorchester, Massachusetts in 1635. His offspring settled throughout New England and into Canada; later my branch of the family ended up on the West Coast, having embraced the Mormon religion. Because the Mormon Church does great genealogy work, I can trace the Millets back to England, and further, to Normandy and the Norman invasion. Hence my father's name was Jean; all of his siblings had French names, although for some reason my grandfather was Artemis.

My great great grandfather was a contemporary of Brigham Young, actually one of his compatriots who had been recruited out of Canada to be a temple builder in Utah. There is a temple (or church), in St. George, Utah, where my wife and I had a house, that honors him as a pioneer temple builder, although we spend more time just down the road from Dorchester, in Boston. As I sit at breakfast with my cup of coffee, I imagine my ancestor Thomas travelling that lone road from Dorchester into Boston—I've come full circle.

I'm essentially a West Coast person born in Los Angeles, raised in Arizona and then California. My grandmother, my father's mother, was born in a covered wagon moving from Utah to northern Arizona, a missionary journey to the Flagstaff area; in those days Mormons were city and community builders. It was Brigham Young's strategy to

1

colonize for the Mormon Church, whereas today the church tries to recruit individual members. My grandmother lived to be one hundred, and died a day before her hundredth birthday (a celebration that turned out to be her funeral). She was somebody I knew well. It's incredible to me that, here we are, putting a Rover on Mars, taking digital photographs, and my grandmother was born in a covered wagon!

My father and I did an interesting trip a few years before he died, visiting his childhood areas. He was sort of orphaned and ended up living with relatives. We went to the community where my grandmother started her life, where her mother died and was buried. Both my parents' large, extended families ended up in Mesa, Arizona, which has a Mormon temple.

My father and mother had both been previously married when they were quite young; theirs was a second marriage. They had known each other in grammar school; my mother was my father's sister's best friend. They met again at a dance and married the next day, which I find strange, since they didn't get along that well. It was just past the Depression; my dad had quit school in the eighth grade, went to California, worked in a feed mill and then a candy mill in Los Angeles, where I was born. When I was young (I was born in 1941), they moved back to Arizona and took over my maternal grandmother's small dairy farm since my dad had grown up on a dairy farm. My first memories are playing on that farm when I was three or four. My father had a real job as a boilermaker on the railroad (my grandmother's father had been a blacksmith on the railroad, in Phoenix). It was the steam engine era when they would repair boilers on steam engines. When my dad's youngest brother went off to war, my dad ran his farm as well as ours. He didn't have to go into the Army because he had what was then a critical job with the railroad. My mother worked as a seamstress. Things were ok.

Everything was going well when the well went dry on my grandmother's farm. No one had the money to drill a new well; my uncle was coming back from the war, so the cows went to him and we moved off the farm. We moved into Mesa to a small rental house. I learned how to swim in Mesa; then things changed again.

The railroads had switched from steam to diesel which meant no more boilers. My dad was given a choice: get laid off or move to the diesel mechanics shop in California. He chose not to stay with the railroad and took a job as a welder in Phoenix, where we moved. He welded the seams of pipes by crawling inside them—they were wide enough for a man, but the heat was extreme. I haven't mentioned my half-brother, who was very ill with polio during that period, and spent time in the hospital suffering through multiple operations. I was going to school but I was on my own a lot. We went to church, and like all Mormons, the extended family was important. They were around to help and there were weekend family gatherings, that sort of thing.

My mom became the head lady in a garment factory when my father was welding pipes. There was a couple from Canada that ran the corner market next to a gas station. My mother would give them a dime a day. I went in after school and could spend that dime on anything I wanted: soda pop, candy bar, anything. They would know I was home from school and watch out for me. Since my mother paid me a penny for a shoebox full of weeds, the dime was ten shoeboxes; that was pretty good. I had a friend who ran a driving range at the country club; I would go and hit golf balls and hang out with him.

To digress, the family had some interesting history. My maternal grandfather shot his brother over my grandmother; he survived, but that resulted in a divorce. Then my grandmother turned around and married the injured brother— we called him Uncle Lon. He had been the head groundskeeper for the city of Phoenix; that was a great thing for me in the summers. They lived on the golf course and I stayed with them. Next door was an amusement park owned by the city—I had free rein to go there and do anything I wanted. I played Little League baseball—my dad was an avid former player and fan—I was on the All Star team. Uncle Lon's son was the school principal; school was great. My friend from the driving range and I rode our bicycles all over town. It wasn't a time when you got into trouble; I have good memories of Phoenix.

When I was ten, my dad went back to work for the railroad in California. We stayed in Phoenix for around four months to pack up and then we moved to Barstow, California, halfway between Los Angeles and Las Vegas, in the middle of nowhere on the Mojave River, where the Santa Fe had their gigantic diesel repair shop. It was at the confluence of the Union Pacific Railroad and the Santa Fe; all the tracks came to Barstow and then split up again—it was a big switching center. My parents bought a house for the first time; I went to school.

My first day, fifth grade in Barstow, was in the middle of

the year, and it was a real shock: a stucco building with an asphalt playground (not like in Phoenix), a chain link fence, no swings. My life changed that day. I had been used to playing sports on green lawns, a baseball field that actually had a grass infield. I was ten turning eleven. The Little League was just starting and the field was dirt and stones. Barstow was in the middle of the desert, hilly, scrubby, honest to god creosote high desert. I was big for my age (at thirteen I got to over six feet!); in Little League my parents had to carry my birth certificate to show other coaches that I was truly under the age limit of twelve. There was no Pony League in Barstow, nothing between little league and high school; I was in limbo for four or five years; being very sports oriented, it was hard.

Ironically, I was too big to play junior varsity football when I finally got into the ninth grade; you had to be fifteen to play varsity. That year I ended up on the taxi squad. The school had a system where kids would be bused in from as far as a hundred miles away and they would stay the week. Otherwise it was a pretty traditional regional high school. Sports were what you would expect: football, basketball, baseball, and track. The junior high was physically connected to the high school, so I became water boy and manager for the varsity when I was still in junior high. I watched the practices every day. In high school I ended up winning twelve varsity letters, which even included track. Sports was my life—the coaching was good. School wasn't my life.

Because the school was in the middle of nowhere, a lot of football games included overnight trips. My dad would drive. I played center on offense because I wasn't terribly fast; I played nose tackle and tight end on defense. It was brutal work but I was good. Senior year the coach said, "You're the first person to go through this program who has the potential to play professional football." I didn't do poorly in school because I was innately pretty smart, but I didn't work hard; I didn't study. When I look back on my childhood, I wish I had studied. I took the college prep program but I hadn't done well enough to think of going to college. My parents didn't encourage me to do better; they thought I was doing fine.

On the other hand, my half- brother with polio had a personality like a nail; he was driven—nothing he couldn't do even though he was an invalid on crutches. When I was five and he was ten he went through five years of hell (not lungs thank God—it was his legs). In high school he was class president. He could build anything with his hands, big model airplanes, airborne on wires; he knew how to tear the engines apart. He was the only person I ever met who could take a puzzle apart and instantly put it back together again. After high school he went to horology school in Elgin, Illinois (studying and building watches); he came home and went off again and got an engineering degree. He ended up working for Ford Aerospace, helping to build the Rover for a moon landing (he became a star in that field!).

For a couple of years my mother was a housewife: she had lady friends and they would sunbathe, or shop and cook dinner. Through a neighbor's husband who was an interior designer, she started making drapes for a building boom that was going on (these were tiny houses but the owners bought furniture and drapes). She eventually rented a house which she converted into a drapery factory, making draperies for a series of decorators. She was a real dynamo; no grass grew under her feet. She even kept a little shop where we lived.

Both my parents were good lookers; my dad was known for his dancing; some said he was a lady's man—it was the big band era. My grandparents on my mother's side lived down in the San Bernardino area; we would go there on weekends and see our cousins. My father's family was still in Arizona; we mostly lost contact with them. That was sad because I really liked my uncles.

My father, now the diesel mechanic, wasn't making great money so he took on a second job moving furniture for a moving and storage company; he got his chauffeur's license so he could drive a moving van. The railroad had three shifts; his job was two weeks on each shift, a crazy lifestyle, especially working the second job and trying to find time to sleep. When he worked graveyard shift, he often managed to work full days at the second job. When it was swing shift time, he might not be able to work for the moving company at all. On a good day, he was able to take short van trips with furniture (the moving company was part of the Mayflower Van Lines). In California you couldn't have certain jobs if you were under sixteen, but when I was fourteen I was big enough to move furniture. I would go with my father or separately, mainly during the summer (everyone thought I was a lot older than I was; by then I was six foot three and weighed one ninety!). If a Mayflower van came to town, they hired locals to help unload; I was one of those locals.

I had a long term relationship in high school. I worked at the movie theatre taking tickets and setting up the marquee, working at the counter, carrying the film cans upstairs to the projection booth. That's how I met Nancy, at the theatre. She had just moved into town; it was love at first sight. She was a year younger; her father was a dentist, a Stanford graduate, an arrogant, bigoted man. I was determined that she was going to be my girlfriend but her father didn't think much of me—I was just a jock. When I graduated, she had one more year of school.

When I look back, I see myself always vacuuming up the old and moving forward—that's what the years look like. I got out of high school in '59, an exceptional football and baseball player, no grades to go anywhere. UCLA wanted me to play football, but there was no way I was going to UCLA, except that they had a totally illegal farm system. A junior college over the hill from UCLA in Riverside that played their style of football took me in and gave me a scholarship.

I had been working for an ice company summers (my dad worked there too). It was a great job, moving 300-pound blocks of ice to the ice house at Fort Irwin, a desert tank training facility in the middle of nowhere 40 miles away—110 degrees in the shade. We would load a flatbed truck, wrap the ice in blankets, head off across the desert, unload, go back and do it again. When I wasn't doing that I took ice to the Santa Fe boxcars.

Then off I went to Riverside Junior College to play football and started going to class. What a change! At Riverside I rented a room and had meals at the house of a woman who would not let you drink milk with fish; of course I was a big milk drinker. Her idea of a meal was fish sticks with vegetables from a can. My scholarship paid for tuition and books, and unlike other scholarship students, I wasn't assigned a campus job.

The football team played me at center on offense and tight end on defense. I weighed 215 and was 6'3". We had two practices a day, real serious football; it was a totally different kind of game than playing in high school. One year before, the college had been sixth ranked junior college in the nation; kids in the Riverside program, from all over California, were football players who couldn't get into a four year college. They were animals, and mean—not all of them, but some. After the first or second game, a few weeks into the season, I realized this was not for me; it was not what I was going to do with my life. I wasn't going to be a jock; I just didn't care for the extra aggressive quality of college football, and I wasn't good enough to play college basketball. I realized I had to do something; I had to change. But I played and we did really well—it was a big deal: top ten team (even my uncles would come to the games). We had a running back who had been in the Air Force; it turned out he was ineligible so we had to forfeit all the games he played in! The quarterback, and others, went on to play major college football; I finished the year and my parents were proud of me.

I didn't go back; I went to Barstow Junior College in their first or second year of operations, stayed at home for a year, started hitting the books and actually did well—first time I'd ever studied in my life. Ironically, the campus was on the

Barstow high school campus. I played basketball and baseball just for something to do. I wasn't an A student but I did ok. I really liked botany, so I thought maybe I'd be a botanist, but I wasn't good at math. A teacher of historical geology was first rate; the desert was a wonderful place to study geology, so we went on field trips every week, to great die-for places. Then I thought it might be fun to be a biologist. One thing for sure: I knew I wasn't going to be a football player, so I knew I wasn't going to finish college on a football scholarship. I had broken up with my girlfriend and she had gone off to the University of California at Davis. She was a good student and was seeing someone else, but I decided I wanted to patch things up and get back together; it was a five hour drive up to Davis.

The next summer I was working again at the ice plant. Nancy came home for the summer; she worked as a dental assistant for her father. We were going out and she was seeing the other guy also. At some point she and her father, a brutal man, came to blows; she hit him with a frying pan—she had had enough. She came to my mother's business as a place of refuge. My mother called me at work to come home—there was a problem. A week later we were married, which was dumb (I'm finishing junior college and she has just finished her freshman year at university!) But we didn't see any other way out. We'd been together a long time; it seemed like the thing to do. We had a wedding; uncle Lon came down from Riverside to marry us. Her father and mother and her siblings all came.

I wasn't signed up to go to school the following year, but one day I was reading a magazine called American Artist (looking back, I had aced all the craft courses in high school: carving, wood shop, all those kinds of things, and could do anything with my hands, like my mother and my brother, so I guess there was interest I was not aware of). I am thumbing through this magazine and there's a little ad for the San Francisco Art Institute: Come to the San Francisco Art Institute and take Commercial Art (not even a full size ad but a little side column ad). I guess I called them because the internet wasn't around—send me the brochures. The brochures came with an application: forward your transcripts. So, what the heck, I ordered my transcripts from Riverside and Barstow, and I'll be damned, they let me in. I was shocked—I hadn't even sent a portfolio! Maybe they liked the fact that I had done all the academic courses you have to take in art school: history and basic science, etc.

San Francisco Art Institute is an affiliate school of UC Berkeley; it's a good education, on Nob Hill in an old Spanish style building. Nancy wanted to return to school in Davis, which was not far from San Francisco. I was pleased to follow; I was getting out of Barstow! The way it ended up, she went to work as a dental assistant on Bush Street at the foot of Nob Hill (the Hyde Street cable car ran right in front of the office). We lived in a little apartment, and I... well, it was such a big change, a huge change. My life history started in San Francisco, or so it seemed for a country bumpkin from an athletic background, poorly educated (I had never read a novel in high school). Suddenly I am going to one of the most prestigious art institutes in the country!

My mother said she would give me a hundred dollars a

month, which paid for my tuition and supplies; this was around 1961-62. Nancy worked; I worked in the summer, but after my first semester I got a full scholarship, because it turned out I was good (I still had to pay for my books and supplies). I was taking Commercial Art—I was an excellent designer. I did well in my painting classes, although to this day I don't think I can paint (I was better at straight lines, drafting and design kind of stuff, color theory—I took to it). I had a mentor my first year, Jim Robertson, an English major from Berkeley who had given up writing and gone into being a designer (he designed the magazine Art Forum which is still exactly as he designed it). His firm was Robertson/ Montgomery in San Francisco. Later he created a fine press publishing house called Yolla Bolly; he died unexpectedly in 2001, but the press continues today under the leadership of his wife Carolyn.

James Robertson changed my life; he taught me how to think, to investigate stuff, how to attack a problem, how not to be lazy about things; I was tenacious. I spent every spare moment at San Francisco Public Library (the big one near city hall) which had a great art book section. I just pored over magazines like Graphics and Industrial Design, anything I could get my hands on. It all fascinated me. It was what I was studying at school but I wanted to know everything and I wanted to see how real people did it. When Jim Robertson came and took over the Commercial Art department, the institute was comprised of photo, sculpture, painting, and graphics (printmaking) schools. He changed Commercial Art to Graphic Design, even if you still had to take courses in all the areas. The only required academic course I didn't have from junior college was Art History, so I had time for the public library, since I didn't have to go over to the state university where my fellow students took science classes.

In commercial art under James Robertson you did renderings for ads, lettering, design for books. I was hooked; I took to it because I have a really good eye and I spent a year absorbing it all. A summer program came along that I wasn't chosen for and I talked my way into it. It was for the Tom Dooley Foundation: they did healthcare stuff and had a hospital ship. It was before the Vietnam War in that part of the world. They came to the school to have us redo their entire graphics campaign (logo, typefaces, brochures).

Jim didn't think that much of me, and I was an underclassman, but I was not going to be overlooked. I don't remember what I did: special work, other things... I ended up in the program designing the Tom Dooley logo and typeface. I wasn't the star of the class because there were some really good people, but I participated and won my share of the battles. Jim questioned everything; he made you think. It was exciting because you had to do real stuff for a foundation that really existed.

Before he died in 2001, I wrote Jim to thank him for changing my life; I wrote a long letter on the computer and told him about my progress to that point. I had seen him once or twice over the years and had done a freelance job for him before I moved east, but now I had a company and was established. I spell-checked my computer letter, since I'm a lousy speller, and then I hand copied it on three or four pages.

I wanted it to be personal (I can write like an architect, which I learned in one of my classes). He was way up in northern California near the Oregon border running the Yolla Bolly Press, publishing his fine art books; he'd sort of dropped out of society. He sent me back a nice note, apologized for not hand-writing it—he was impressed I had taken the time. He said, "I was only a few steps ahead of you guys the whole time at school; it was all new to me too. Some of you were so good."

First rate designers came out of that class at the San Francisco Art Institute (Stewart Brand who did the Whole Earth Catalog, Michael Manwaring the great graphic designer, a couple of illustrators: Jerry Reis and Charley Fleischman). Jim also brought in great teachers because that was the group he ran around with.

When I look back I realize I was so absorbed in the new world I had discovered I was neglecting Nancy, although at the time it wasn't apparent to me. I learned after my second marriage to pay attention. After that summer I found photography: the Ansel Adams system—it was his program. He had retired, but his protégées were running a serious workshop, which again was absolutely different from the world I had come from. I just sucked it up (his zone system for instance). I started doing my design projects for Jim centered around photography. Then I became interested in solving things three dimensionally. I would do a photographic sculpture solution, make a poster up. I was adapting my skills, not that I wanted to change my career; I was a designer who was taking pictures with a Nikon F (I worked a deal with a

Japanese classmate to have his stewardess sister bring in the camera). 3D stuff, photography, I was even doing some painting, all of which in the end fed into graphic design. I would do a drawing in life class, in pencil on thick paper, and I took white tempera and painted everywhere except where the lines were. Then I stretched it, and coated it with india ink. Finally I took a hose and hosed off the tempura; it looked just like a lithograph. I made decent money selling artwork.

Gordon Ashby came to San Francisco and set up an office while I was still a student; he was an exhibit designer out of the Charles Eames office in Venice, California (people tend to remember Eames for the Eames chair). Gordon started with an IBM project (IBM had been Eames' biggest client). He had contracted hepatitis working on the New York World's Fair for Eames. IBM gave him a project and Eames gave him permission to take it and leave the office. Gordon was Jim Robertson's age; they were friends. He came to teach at the school to make some extra money and needed a student helper; Jim knew I was interested in 3D things and was a hard worker. I got my portfolio together and visited Gordon's office near the school. I started showing him my portfolio and he said" "Do you want a job or not?" I put my book away and got the job, another life changer: Suddenly I was in the big league design world of IBM and Charles Eames.

Immediately we started working on Astronomia, an IBM sponsored exhibit at the Hayden Planetarium of the American Museum of Natural History in New York City. It was an exhibit on the history of astronomy. I was still in school, getting my Master's in painting and I had been put on this full time job! The writer on Astronomia was Stewart Brand, later the Whole Earth Catalogue guy, who had just gone through the same program I was in at the Art Institute, a biologist from Stanford who wanted to know design. He was writing the history of astronomy for Gordon. A rarefied atmosphere? For a kid a few years out of junior college in Barstow, California, just getting by, planning not to play football, to big league graphic designer in New York City, it was mind boggling. Thank God I found this world, as I said to Jim in my letter.

It turned out that in this corner of the exhibit design world, you had to do all those things I was studying, and also be able to deal with clients. The approach of the Eames office, and the office set up by Gordon Ashby, was multi-disciplinary. As the Eames office was finishing up the New York World's Fair, Gordon farmed me out to take pictures, because extra help was needed. I'm running around L.A. taking pictures for Charles Eames (for the New York World's Fair in '64 and '65), still wet between the ears and doing it as if I am a veteran photographer!

Gordon redid Astronomia a few years later when it had to be refurbished and updated, and asked me to come back and work on it; we went to New York to put in our installations separately because, by that time, we couldn't get along, but he needed me to do the job, a sad commentary on creativity. I went to the recent movie on Charles Eames, and there was Gordon, forty years later on the screen, close-up, a spokesperson for his mentor.

I was at the San Francisco Art institute three and a half years, and with the two junior colleges, five and a half years of higher education. At graduation, I was the only one wearing a suit (this was San Francisco pre-hippie days). My parents came; it was a big deal. Our school band played: it was a student rock group, Big Brother and the Holding Company (Janis Joplin was part of it—Dave Getz, a painter, was the drummer). For the last time my two worlds sort of came together.

Nancy and I were now living in Marin County, in the last house bordering Mount Tamalpais, having bought a VW from her boss; Nancy was still working but was back at school in Berkeley studying to become a marine biologist. She ended up leaving me, and I don't blame her. I have already mentioned I was preoccupied, and responsible, although she was partly to blame. I found out later she dropped out of a doctorate program, eventually moving to New York with a new husband, an attorney, having been involved with a married professor with five children that didn't end well. Later, she ran a good sized New York company in Times Square before moving back out west—she was a bright lady.

Getting into the design world, you had to be a graphic artist, a photographer; you had to be able to write, to do sound, deal with clients. I was working around the clock, going off on trips a lot, because that's the nature of the business. Gordon Ashby brought in a series of good jobs. Kevin Roche, formerly a senior designer with Eero Saarinen, and John Dinkeloo, an architect, opened up their own architecture office when Saarinen died and they designed the Oakland Museum. Through the Eames connection (Eames and Saarinen were best friends), they engaged Gordon to do the exhibit design.

Gordon also brought in other work: an IBM pavilion at the Montreal World's Fair in '67, and a State of Texas pavilion at Hemisphere '68 in San Antonio.

Because the Olympics were in Mexico City, San Antonio thought they would get a lot of residual traffic, but it didn't happen. However, the city was rebuilt around the fair. We did the State of Texas pavilion for John Connolly, who was then the governor of Texas. I headed up the film side while Gordon did the exhibits. My side was a 25 projector film about the history of Texas. What I didn't know about filmmaking I learned very quickly on the job. I remember sitting in a restaurant in San Antonia with Gordon. On a napkin (Gordon was impressive—he could really draw), he drew a dome with screens on the inside of the dome. It was his vision of what we were going to do in a gymnasium size hall. It turned out to be a movie going back to the early days in Texas when contractors would bring in Hungarian workers, Danes, Germans, signifying the fact that there are different cultures in Texas even up to the present day. We did a 35mm film, sound, three cameras, the works, shot panoramas simultaneously. We had to invent a machine that ran film at the same speed, incorporating selsyn (self-synchronous) motors. When you sent current to the projectors, it grabbed magnets which allowed the projectors to run in sync. So you could actually run different films with the assurance they were, in effect, on the same frame. You had the rodeo going, and the bucking horse was going from screen to screen in the dome. Gordon had seen something like this at the New York World's Fair; he thought about things, but I made them happen, which is why we really worked well together.

I'm still well under thirty—I'm divorced (I can't say I wasn't hurt). I'm busy, running around in a station wagon with a film crew in Texas. John Connolly is coming to the office in California to see screenings in his motorcade (this is after he has been shot during the Kennedy assassination, so he's a fairly famous man). We had to make a mock-up of a dome, piece it together for him; he liked it—we finished it. It worked (I can't believe it worked; it was so complicated, way more complicated than what we should have tried). We never heard any complaints.

When you walk out the door at the end of a project, it's gone, history. It's that vacuuming up thing I mentioned earlier. Whether it ran or didn't run during the six months it was on, I have no idea. You are already on to the next one. And that's sort of what life is for me also. Some people live for their histories, for their memories; I don't. Some of us move on and don't look back. I break my life into segments. Prior to just a few years ago San Francisco was the beginning segment. I just didn't tell anyone about prior to San Francisco, which was my coming out time. Now I say I'm from Barstow. People laugh and we have a little joke about it, because it's notorious as a dead-end place; everyone in California knows Barstow. You go to Las Vegas you go through Barstow. "How did you get out (chuckle)?" I still don't tell anyone about high school and sports, or my nickname in high school (Lefty). I look at my retirement from my company, selling it, and what I am doing now as two entirely different segments, and I don't correspond with anyone from my company.

Gordon had sort of promised me I would become a partner in his firm. He needed me; I was an integral part of his effort. I was running several people, doing this film. Of course he was free to look at it from a bigger picture; without question he was a genius. So now Osaka is coming up next on the World's Fair circuit; I assume we're going to get it. He comes in one day, after we wrapped up Texas, and he announces he's closing the office and going to Mexico for a year and doesn't know what he's going to do when he comes back! I had just lost my marriage, working non-stop, travelling, "How can you do this?" That was my reaction. But Gordon closed the office and gave me two hundred dollars severance. A few years later he asked for the two hundred dollars back, said it was a loan! It was weird.

Fortunately I had a few things going; I was dabbling in freelance as a photographer-filmmaker. But I had to find more work. Jim Robertson gave me some assignments, but I was really out on the street trying to scrape together my life. I took photographs and started eking out a living the best way I could with assignments that were few and far between. I found a publisher in New York, Houghton Mifflin, doing a series of kid's educational books, in which they needed photographs of kid's doing things. It was a program in which teachers in the inner city tried to get students to interact with the photographs and with each other. Jim Robertson recommended me to the woman who was running the project. It was a yearlong gig, shooting in San Francisco, L.A., New York, and Chicago.

Shooting in New York in the middle of winter, it was cold, and I had no winter clothes, just a Levi jacket. I got my two hundred dollar expense check from Houghton Mifflin and went into Abercrombie and Fitch, which at that time was a high end sports clothing and expedition/safari store; I bought a big fur parka. I put it on, walked down Fifth Avenue—I was warm. It was all the money I had; I still have that coat.

I was doing street photography during the same period because I wanted to be an artist. I tried to take a good photograph each day for a year, at the end of which I put together a portfolio of the best thirty to thirty-five shots, printed them small, and put them in a nice box. There was a magazine in Switzerland called Camera, the best photo magazine in the world. I sent that box to the editor—he got it and within an hour was on the phone, wanting to publish the portfolio, which he did. I had sent the box to him as a gift because I liked his magazine; that's what I said in a note. All of a sudden I'm an artist! They paid me but not much.

I'm still in San Francisco, but I'm burning friends, burning relationships. I now have a girlfriend who became my second wife: Kay (she passed away this last year which was sad). I'm not getting along with her because she's doing other stuff, so I decide I'm going to move to New York. Alan Porter, of Camera, sends me a note saying they are doing an issue on California photographers: Could I send him some stuff, just color. I send him a couple sleeves of slides.

I packed Nancy's Volkswagen which she now wanted in New York (it was still in California even though we had been divorced for some time). Then I drove to New York with almost everything I owned. I had my cameras, my clothes, and six hundred dollars in my pocket. I went to Michael Ross, an architect—his wife's name was Anna (he had lived above me in San Francisco when I lived in the North Beach area; once when I was really broke he gave me two hundred dollars). He was a really nice guy, younger than me, worked for Skidmore, Owens in New York and lived on 10th Street in the Village. I had called and asked if I could stay with them. I showed up with Nancy's Volkswagen, and the first thing Anna said was, "How long are you staying?" In my California way I said:,"I don't know—I guess until I get something happening." By that evening Michael said, "You've got two days."

I went down the street to a flophouse hotel, above an Automat. I had a few Nikons, several Hasselblads with me, lenses (I was carrying several thousand dollars of camera gear and I was in a flophouse in Greenwich Village!). I was shooting photographs and trying to get work, so I made a deal with the guy at the front desk. My gear would go under the desk and he would watch it. I realize now I could have lost everything but I stayed awhile and ate at the Automat. There were lots of old people who came in there, got their sandwiches, and were eating all alone, and I thought: I'm not sure I want to be in New York at that age. There is a song: "Froggy Comes a Courtin'," a hit at the time. Every time it came on the radio, the guy in the room next door at my flophouse would masturbate, singing at the top of his voice to the music. This happened several times a day.

I had my connection with the publisher Houghton Mifflin: the children's book editor Susan Windsor. She put me in contact with a guy who was working on some Sesame Street textbook stuff, and I tried to get a living going. She also knew a woman who was going to Europe for six months who had a sixth floor walk-up on 66th Street off York. Would I like to rent until she came back? Of course I took it even though I didn't know how I was going to pay (anything to get away from Froggy Comes a Courtin'). Across the street was an elegant apartment building where the hookers would come and go, upscale East side hookers. I sat on the fire escape and watched them come and go. Then Kay decided she wanted to come to New York and the woman was about to come back from Europe.

Susan Windsor knew a couple in New Jersey who were renting in an old mill building complex in Edgewater, below the cliffs by the Hudson River. If I would do carpentry work, there was another space in which we could live. The other couple, a photographer and his wife were nice people, and they were also working on the building. The owner was a Cornell professor who liked artists, so the complex was full of misfits who were handy. The guy who kind of ran the place was a school teacher. I moved in and Kay arrived; we decided to get married, at the Edgewater fire station, by a Justice of the Peace: wife number two, actually an East Coast person from Pennsylvania. Her father had been a football coach under Bear Bryant in Alabama and then a head coach in Indiana, Pennsylvania, where she went to high school; she still had a southern accent, and of course we met in California, where she started as a school teacher, dropped out, did lots of drugs, and liked me because I was an artist. In New Jersey she started doing fabric sculpture and was very good at it: unbelievable crochet work.

We were struggling economically; the textbook work ran out, so I was doing carpentry to pay the rent. I used to walk across the George Washington Bridge and take the subway downtown looking for work. I got a job at Modern Age Photo Lab. I was a good black and white printer, showed the guy my printing in the portfolio. He said, "We have a little test here for our printers." He gave me three problematic negatives and sent me into a darkroom to make a print of each negative: five minutes a print. I didn't pass the test, but he gave me a film processing job. They had a big room with tanks; you would take 200 rolls of black and white film, turn the lights off—pitch black, totally black—pop open a canister, put a weight on each end of the individual film and hang it on a rack hanger, 200 rolls of film. You would then lower these hangers into the tanks, start the timer (remember: no light except a clock on the wall with luminous hands, and even that was covered except when you were timing). Modern Age Photo Lab's claim to fame? They processed your film through inspection. How was that done? You took a green light, not film sensitive, held the film up and gauged how far you were in processing, put it back in the tank and did 200 rolls, sometimes 250 rolls. It was a completely bogus process, and the job was horrible: doing this all day long, I lasted two months.

That's when I said I've got to get a job with my graphic design background, because photography is not going to pay the bills—that's an art. A woman who worked under me for Gordon Ashby in San Francisco had a good friend, a college roommate named Rita Sue Sigel in New York. She had the largest graphic arts recruiting firm in the city, and recruited designers and architects for all the best places.

I called Rita Sue, who I had met in San Francisco, and she remembered me (again, fortuitous). She had a guy on Madison Avenue who needed help, not a great job, but she said I should take it and she would keep looking. I went up to interview; Jim looked at my portfolio; it flipped him out, all this World's Fair stuff. He needed a three dimensional guy to do some work on a Pan Am project, so he hired me. It was him, the woman who answered the phone and made appointments, and me. He had been the partner in a famous design firm; his partner had finally gotten tired of his drinking (he was a down and out drunk), so they split up. Here he was, on his own, and he had this Pan Am connection.

I went to work every day and tried to solve a window display problem for Pan Am with the woman who answered the phone, because we had nothing else to do. He would go out in the morning and come back so drunk he would lie down on the couch and go to sleep. Pan Am had something they wanted duplicated but actually... not duplicated—I was having no luck. Every Friday Jim came in with cash and paid me under the table. This went on for five or six weeks, long enough that it was boring. He kept saying he was going out to get more work and he didn't want to lose me—I was the caliber he needed, but he never got more work, and he kept drinking.

Then Rita Sue called and said Corning Glass needed a designer; was I interested? I said, "You mean over on 5th Avenue?" No, it was in Corning, New York. "Where is that?"

She said upstate New York. I said I would ask Kay and Kay
didn't want to do it, but they were going to pay my way up
there for an interview, feed me, pay my hotel, so I went; it
would be a fun trip. I told Jim, my drunk employer, I was sick,
but it turned out this was the famous hurricane of '72. It
rained; there was a massive flood in Corning.

I went up to Corning for the weekend, was wined and
dined, showed them my stuff—they wanted me, and there I
was in my sandals and pony tail, no proper clothes—I had
none except for white linen pants, no suit coat. Kay didn't
want to move up there; it reminded her too much of rural
Pennsylvania. But Corning had a great program, one of the top
design programs in the country, everything they touched, and
they had good people working there. In the cubicles were
people from South Africa, from all over the world. I went back
to Kay and said, "I can't not take this job; we're broke." They
paid for both of us to come up, for her to see. The place was
an absolute wreck from the flood, devastated. But I took the
job and they paid to move us, which wasn't much, and due to
the flood there was no place to live (people were living in
trailers). Short term, they put us in a little room upstairs in
somebody's house.

I went to work every day; Kay had nothing to do, but she
decided she wanted to live in the country. She said, "I want to
live in an abandoned school house." We went looking for a
school house. Eventually we found a house on the river,
actually on a creek at the end of a two mile dirt road that had
been a hunting lodge, a summer hunting lodge fifteen miles
out of town. They wanted five thousand dollars. It had no

electricity, no insulation or heat, no water, and there was no house closer than two miles, except across the river where you could see a highway and some houses. We had no money, but we were able to get a mortgage because I was working for Corning. We bought my New Jersey landlord's blue Land Rover with a loan from a credit union and moved in, in October.

The first year was survival—all we had for heat was a potbelly stove; I cut forty cords of wood that winter. I found some cloth drapes from an old exhibit and hung them off the ceiling in a circle in the living room, around the big potbelly, floor to ceiling, and we slept in that space—we did everything we could do there, even brought in a tin washtub to bathe. By the second winter I had insulated, and at some point we got a better stove and purchased a heater.

When we got up in the morning that first year, the dog's water in the kitchen was frozen solid. I was up at four and went out with the chainsaw and an ax; I cut wood for that day's heat before going to work. At night I started fixing the house, a monumental undertaking, but in the end we had water, electricity, and even a phone; the second year we had a toilet (and got rid of the outhouse). I worked full time and I worked on the house. That was the rule: work on the house daily. The whole inside of the house was shiplap pine, beautiful. I took every piece down, numbered it, put each one back in order: insulation, wiring, did this forever.

Kay had been credentialed as a Montessori teacher and started teaching at a Montessori school. She eventually took over the school, when Peggy, the owner, decided she didn't want to do it full time. Later, she got back to her crocheting and opened a yarn store in Corning, which was kind of the downfall of our marriage, because she spent a lot of time in the bar across the street. In retrospect, I think you could classify her as an alcoholic; she passed away recently, and I think that was the reason.

Bob Ivers was my boss at Corning; he fancied himself a good designer because he knew how to pick and edit designs and how to work with good people. He ran a fine program. I did my design stuff; I travelled, worked exhibits and trade shows. I knew I could do photography; I started doing pictures. I had clients, and clients loved me. I solved people's problems. They kind of liked me being a misfit. There was a Corning Consumer's Group of designers; Steuben, a sister company, had designers. Bob had a rule: once a month you had to get on the company jet, go to New York and spend at least two days, on the company, to keep you connected culturally (he knew how isolated it was in upstate New York).

If there was a seat on the company jet you could go anywhere it was going. No kids were allowed on the plane, but your wife could go. If it was headed for New York, the plane landed at Teterboro Airport; a limo was there to meet the Chairman or Vice Chairman, but that limo would take you into Manhattan to wherever you were going. I went to New York on business because my exhibit houses were in New York.

Corning Glass had a media center that produced little films about the company, that did all the company photography. Bob had hired me, thinking maybe I could fit into that effort; he didn't have a spot there at the time, but he knew he wanted to change the guy running it, because that guy was old school and wasn't taking it anywhere. But the man was a friend of the Houghton's, the prominent owners (Arthur Houghton had been on the board of the Metropolitan in New York; he was a Steuben Houghton). Eventually Bob sent me over to run the group, to make it more productive for the company, upgrade it. In doing that, I met my future business partner.

My wife Kay met Bruce Lehman first, when he brought his son to the Montessori school. He smelled bad, had a beard, long hair, and happened to live in the same community. He enrolled his son in the school and got to talking to Kay; she asked him what he did. He said he was a writer, a house husband and a farmer who had gone to Rutgers to become a writer (he didn't tell her he was Phi Beta Kappa). She said, "Oh, my husband uses writers; why don't you go see him." She came home all excited because she met this interesting person who said he would call me. I didn't expect a call but he called and came in, said he was a writer; it was timely.

Corning was working on a project for the space shuttle: a glass coating for the windows. I told him we were doing a moon launch project, a little film, "I need a writer for it." He said, "Oh, I can do that." I gave him a synopsis of the project; he went off. A couple days later he came back. It was so bad I just beat the shit out of him. He didn't know about film, he didn't know about sequencing—it was literature; there was no visual content. He went off—we did this three or four times and it got better each time—he never complained or had an ego thing, and he never took a bath (he always smelled bad). Marylou, who ran the group—the administrator, when he left, said, "Oh my god, don't let him come back, he smells so bad." We did the film; as I recall it was pretty awful, but we worked well together (I didn't have to do the nitty-gritty; he didn't have to do the big thinking). He worked hard; I worked hard. We started doing a few projects, even slide shows, cleaned him up and got him connected with some of my clients.

Corning wanted to do a book about their worldwide effort; they wanted a photographer to go shooting around the world. I said I'm not hiring someone; I'm going to do that myself. I kind of manipulated the system to the extent that I got the assignment, even though I was running things at the Media Center. I gave Bruce, a freelancer, the job of finishing everything we were doing, even though he didn't know how to do anything but write!

I got my gear together and stepped on a plane, went around the world: three and a half months of travel. Kay went with me to Scotland, England, and France (the first three legs). She hung out in Europe on her own for a while; I went to Italy. Bruce, God bless him, somehow kept it all together on the home front. I lugged strobe lights, everything, no assistant (we were on a tight budget). If I had hired a photographer for a job like that, he would have insisted on an assistant. I went to Corning installations worldwide and shot, went to companies like Mercedes Benz, the idea being to photograph the specific Corning product used on the vehicle with a Mercedes Benz, in that case the catalytic converter. The effort was to show clients and prospective customers Corning products in action. I went to Brazil and Japan, China and Korea; I shot some of our glass products.

When I came back, Bruce was still there; Kay was at our home. The designers started putting a book together; Corning decided they didn't want to show any other company logos in the book. They went through all my work to systematically eliminate what had been the purpose of my trip: to show Corning with their customers. But the book was published (it was a major undertaking).

Not long after the project was completed Bruce and I asked the same question: Why are we doing this for the company? We had customers, a media center with divisional people who effectively hired us to do projects. Of course I came free of charge, being an employee. But why not go over to Market Street (in Corning), hire space, open a business, do what we're doing now: design, media stuff. Gordon Ashby, way back when, taught me this trick: If you want to set up a business, the first thing to do is get a project before you leave, and be so indispensable to that job, you take it with you—it will put you in business. That's what Gordon did with IBM and Astronomia when he left Eames. We had to take a job with us to set up an office, since neither one of us had any capital.

Amo Houghton, who became a Congressman from New York, and was the Chairman of Corning, wanted to do a film about the company. Bob Ivers, my boss, said, "You guys are going to do a film about the company." So Bruce and I interviewed Amo and produced a scenario. We laid it all out in just over a month, got Amo hooked on the film (Bruce and Amo hit it off wonderfully). I went in to Bob Ivers and resigned. I said, "And by the way, I'm taking the film with me because Amo wants me to finish it" Bob Ivers was livid, but he only had two choices: start over with a new filmmaker and writer, or let us do the film. I had been at Corning just about seven years.

I always tell the story as if I'm proud of it; I'm not sure I am, but we took the project, rented space at 27 East Market Street, upstairs over an insurance company, and kept working on the film. Corning decided to pay for the film in advance, because they didn't want the cost to spill over into the next year. They gave us a check for the total project; we took that check to the bank and deposited it in a commercial account. They were overjoyed to have us as a customer, and gave us a loan to start the business. We still had the money to do the film, and started LehmanMillet Incorporated with the loan, which Bruce and I ran for thirty years.

We did the movie, made easier because we had established relationships with all the businesses. We had previously befriended their general managers, because of our work with the media center. They liked me, they liked Bruce, so we started going to them to get other work. They would send us to their marketing people for projects. Of course Bob Ivers never gave us a job even though he hired freelancers all the time (I found out recently that he inquired about me to a mutual friend and reminisced about me in positive terms).

Work for the Corning general managers started with slide shows. Each GM had to go to the Board of Directors and formally present his business; it was on a rotation basis. We got Bill Hudson who ran a Corning company that made technical products, a lot of hotshot stuff, to make a multi-screen presentation to the Board in New York (he was enamored with our dynamite technology). Bill was a great guy and wowed them. This started a one-upmanship series of presentations by the other division managers; each one wanted to outdo the previous manager. Bruce and I started creating slide shows three months ahead of board meetings. It seemed we had a new multi-screen slide show ready every three months; we built a business on it. We did other stuff, but this was our staple. We rented another floor, put in a photo lab, processed all of our own film and purchased animation machines.

We started hiring in 1978 or 1979: Lark, my present wife, came to work for us. She and her husband Marty, a lawyer, had moved to Corning from New York City; he was hired to work for the Legal Services Group at Corning (they eventually split up). A Parsons graduate, Lark needed a job and was a capable designer; my wife Kay and Lark had met; Kay told her we were going to start the business, and around that time Kay left and moved back to California to work in movies—she loved California. Lark had worked in New York for years and was a real find for us; you didn't find top people in that part of the country, far from the big city.

The business grew; our bank gave us multiple loans but we were pretty much in debt, which a business often is, so we tried to crack Rochester where Kodak was located (we had no success). Corning Medical Division, in Medfield, Massachusetts, became our largest client. They made blood gas monitoring equipment (to measure your blood oxygen), and other medical instruments. Another Corning division had come up with a way for a piece of glass to measure PH, and for a wafer of glass to measure oxygen content. That's how Corning worked; they would come up with innovations that had the potential to become commercial successes. We did a lot of films about the innovations used by the Medical Division in their products. My partner Bruce, who is really smart, got along well with Marty, the CEO of that division; he could understand any of the technical stuff and had a photographic memory, my total opposite (he was Phi Beta Kappa at Rutgers). Bruce and I got along well, but we were two sides of a coin.

We did a gigantic slide show for Marty (the CEO of the Medical Division) to present to the Board of Directors. He was like an entertainer—he was the only VP we did a film for who didn't use a script. He would run without looking at the screen, with several images changing behind him, and deliver the pitch—he was a genius who could present complicated stuff and make it understandable.

One day Amo Houghton, the Chairman of Corning, almost put us out of business. "We're seeing these shows every board meeting," he said, "how much are they costing?" When he was told, that ended it. He said, "Enough—you bring in one slide, you tell us your strategy, that's it."

LehmanMillet moved to Boston in 1984, because there was no future in Corning, New York. We packed up everything, including six or seven key people. We still had Marty as a customer, for whom we did promotional stuff, but we didn't have the slide shows anymore. Lark had left the company and was doing children's books, very successfully, and we were together. Before LehmanMillet left, we went to the bank and took out a big six figure loan; they still loved us because we were profitable and doing a good job from their perspective. But we had a hard time, struggled, almost went bankrupt multiple times between 1984 and 1990. First, Lark and I lived in town, then we bought a house in Duxbury, moved to East Cambridge for a while. Bruce bought a house near Foxboro and was married a second time. Somewhere in there we lost a house to debt, because we had used the house for collateral.

In trying to grow a business, we changed from a media company to an advertising agency specializing in medical. Over time we became the largest device and diagnostic advertising agency in the United States (we didn't do pharmaceutical). After the hard times we started to get better clients: J & J, Hewlett-Packard (they had a medical division), clients in Switzerland and Germany; we opened a branch in London to service and open up Europe and the UK (I did a lot of travelling back and forth). We were never terribly profitable but LehmanMillet became a real business. I was proud of the fact (and said so at my retirement), that in thirty years we never missed a paycheck.

In 1999 Bruce and I realized we had to sell the company if we were going to get anything out of it. We brought in a firm to look at the company, to help sell it, and they said: you really don't have the stature to sell now. "You're paying yourselves well; you run a good clean business: good books—you pay your taxes, but there's no real equity here except goodwill. Take a couple years, get your books in shape, quit spending as much as you bring in." So we did that and firmed up our client base. Then we shopped the company.

I sat on a board that met once a month in New York dealing with the legislative impact of medical advertising. I met Gil Bash, a feisty little guy, a former paratrooper who was running a big PR firm; for some reason we really hit it off. We would sit next to each other at conferences, talk, and he told me at one point that he left his own firm and went to work for the largest medical advertising agency in the country: CommonHealth, a WPP company (the London ad agency conglomerate). He was now President of CommonHealth. At an awards dinner in 2000 at The Plaza in New York (invited to sit at a CommonHealth table), I walked out with Gil (it was raining), to smoke a cigar under an umbrella. Gil was about to get into a cab, and I said to him, "Gil, we're thinking of selling the company—do you think you could help me figure out how to do that?" He said, "Don't do anything before you talk to me."

A week or so later Gil called, "I want to talk to you about buying the company. Here's the deal; we want to buy you guys." He had just left CommonHealth to work for an investor in Chicago who was doing a roll-up of medical advertising companies. That fellow was working for an even larger company. Gil knew he wanted our company, but without fail he wanted the two principals: he wanted me and he wanted Bruce (he thought Bruce walked on water). We were the first firm they bought; they even paid for our attorney. We had to stay three years, but it was a good deal. We went to Chicago to meet with the investors and started to work under them.

It wasn't long before we were off to Florida to buy a company—they wanted us to buy smaller medical firms to put under our umbrella. We stayed three days, in Hollywood, Florida, bonded with the principals, and Bruce went to the airport to fly home. I followed a bit later and was looking at the monitor—the World Trade Center was burning—it's 9/11. Bruce's plane turned around and landed. We were in Ft. Lauderdale. Three or four days later Bruce was able to catch a flight because he was willing to fly to Providence. I took a train from Miami to Boston; it was packed, no sleepers, and the toilets were all clogged.

I only repeat the story, which is so familiar to us all, because it was a moment that changed the marketplace. And for the company that bought us, medical turned out to be too ethereal, not what they were used to, which was nuts and bolts. They had chosen a business that was just not compatible with their experience. They had done things like roll up laundromats and auto supply stores. We were intellectual property and goodwill; they decided they didn't want to continue with the roll-up. Because of 9/11 the Florida thing went nowhere.

After a year and a half, our owners asked us to help them sell the company. They were willing to cover any difference between what we sold the company for and what they had contractually agreed to pay us. They could have thrown us out on the street—it was a good deal: nice guys.

Bruce was good at selling; we did a dog and pony show in New York, for fifteen potential buyers, got an investment banker to help us, put the thing together. Healthstar

Communications, a start-up, really wanted us. They were building pharmaceutical agencies. The others didn't want to walk across the street for us. Our company in Chicago would not take stock, which Healthstar offered. In the end they paid mostly in cash and a minor amount of stock. They still own the company—Bruce still works there. I stayed three more years, a total of four and a half years. We bought a small agency in California for a West Coast presence. They needed structure, so I ran that company during those three years (I'm a good structural repair guy). An ad agency basically sells time: this agency didn't have a clock, not one clock. First thing I did was send someone to Crate and Barrel to buy fifteen clocks; they went in every room—the conference room got two. That company is now bigger than the company in Boston, both still LehmanMillet. All the principals are gone, except Bruce.

I was going to move to LA, run the company out there; we bought a house in Utah thinking it was close to LA, but I got very sick with Viral Pneumonia (sometimes called Boop). I couldn't work, went on massive doses of steroids for nine months. When that illness finished I never went back to work. But in a sense I had closed the loop.

I started WALLWORK the gallery.

Mary Putnam Post Chatfield

Known as Polly, a wonderful mother and volunteer, devoted teacher and writer

I never knew my grandfathers; they died long before I was born. I knew my father's mother, my grandmother, though she died when I was four. She had illustrious siblings: her brother Percival Lowell founded the Lowell Observatory (his initials were used to name the once-planet Pluto); her brother A. Lawrence Lowell was president of Harvard; her sister was the poet Amy Lowell. She had been, in her own right, a crusader for a whole list of causes: the women's vote, pasteurization of milk, the repeal of prohibition. Her husband was a lawyer in Boston, but they decided it would be much better for their children not to be in the city. They moved to Manchester and he took the train to Boston every morning.

When I was three I was taken to Grandmother's house, a big rambling place with a cookie jar in every bedroom; I visited with her, sitting in bed each morning. Whenever I smell the combination of roses and sand the house comes back to me. We walked down a path through a rose trellis to the beach; she told me one morning the foghorn that was blowing was Baby Baker; that appealed to me at three, I don't know why. My great aunt lived somewhere off to the left, and an uncle and aunt were to the right.

My father and mother met during the First World War. My mother, Caroline Piatt Jenkins, was from Maryland; her grandfather had been a country doctor who was arrested twice during the Civil War, once for providing medicines to the Confederate Army, and again after the assassination of Lincoln. When someone said how awful it was that a doctor had set John Wilkes Booth's broken leg, my great grandfather said he would have done the same thing; he got clapped into prison!

My father, Roger Lowell Putnam, served in the Navy during the war; that was after Harvard and a year at MIT. He was sent to the Naval Proving Grounds in Indian Head, Maryland, south of Washington, on the east bank of the Potomac where they did testing. He used his engineering degrees and did R & D; his immediate superior became Admiral Kirk in World War II and brought my father to England as a Lieutenant Commander doing R & D for the invasion of France (they were trying out all sorts of amphibian vehicles at the time).

My mother's father had died in 1905 when she was thirteen, in a family of six brothers and one baby sister. My mother was sent to boarding school in Baltimore but after the first two months of ninth grade her mother took her out of school to help at home; that was all the formal schooling she had, though she was determined to be educated (I discovered later she read books I had to read in graduate school). I once asked her what was the hardest subject to learn on her own; she said French, because she forgot how it sounded. With all those brothers she was a very competitive lady.

At twenty-six, Mother was an old maid and a blue stocking. The wife of Admiral Lackey, my father's commandant, asked her to run a tiny lending library on the base (she thought my mother would not be a temptation to the officers). Mother said, "Your father started taking out more books than I knew he could read." He had noticed her driving a whole baseball team in a big Stutz Bearcat car; (she was the first woman in southern Maryland to have a driving license). My father thought this was an interesting woman to know and turned around his car to follow her.

There were parties for the officers, afternoon parties where they played lawn tennis and tag. My mother told her sister (who was with her one fateful day), "You can stop running; he's not chasing you." My father eventually proposed to her and she went to her pastor (she was a Roman Catholic) to tell him she had been proposed to by a naval officer, a Northerner, a Republican and not a Roman Catholic. He said, "Caroline, at your age you couldn't get a better offer." Little did he know they were made for each other; the only time I saw my mother cry had nothing to do with my father: it was during the hurricane of '38 when all the trees behind our house blew down. There were six children in my family (I was number five, born in October of 1929).

My parents were married during October of 1919 in Baltimore in a cousin's house; they went north to Springfield, Massachusetts, where my father became a Democrat rather quickly and started Packaging Machinery Company in 1921 (I believe he had financial help from his father). He manufactured machines that wrapped different colored cellophane tops onto the cardboard tops of milk bottles, machines that wrapped and added pull-tape for Chiclet chewing gum and Hershey's kisses. They eventually had contracts with Birdseye (the frozen food company), Beechnut, Mars (for Mars bars), and many others. It became a big business; during WWII the company was very active in the war effort.

I can remember family life was orderly; my mother had plenty of domestic help. There was a cook, a chambermaid, a sort of nursemaid, and outside help. The home they moved to on Central Street when I was born was a big brick house that had a huge carriage house much larger than a normal garage. Fred had the job of watching the stove to keep the carriage house warm; he had been a drummer boy in the Civil War and lived in the old soldier's home; it was a way of giving him something to do and some money to spend.

My mother was a devout Roman Catholic; my father was not. They agreed, however, that all the children would have a Catholic education through high school; the boys would then go to Harvard and the girls would attend a Catholic college. I went to the St. Michael's Cathedral Grammar School, which was our parish, then to Sacred Heart Convent and Sacred Heart College in Newton. In the wintertime when I was still at home, our father always went to church with us, and in the summer when we were in Petersham (50 miles north of Springfield, near the great Quabbin Reservoir), he wanted to be in the woods (my mother, however, asked him not to use the chain saw while we were in church so that no one would know he was out in the woods!). In those days everyone was afraid of polio, including our mother, who wanted us out of the city during the summer when polio was contracted (no one knew how it was spread). Off we went to Petersham; we never went to the movies—we never did anything in a crowd starting in late May, though we did go to church. Over the years my parents rented several different houses in Petersham, and then they built a three story shingle house with a swimming pool in the woods. My mother always served tea in the afternoon to all the children and our friends who came to swim, who had to be out of the pool and dressed for tea, no exceptions (you had tea and then went home). My mother lived to be one hundred; she died November 16th, 1992, outliving my father by twenty years (not bad for an old maid!)

We were a lively intellectual family; my parents read to us every night, sometimes in a family group, sometimes the little ones in bed. If you were old enough, after supper in the living room you played spelling or geography games or learned how to knit, or sat with my father to do the crossword puzzle (he taught me how to do diagram-less puzzles!). It was then our parents read to us, Dickens, Kipling and Thackeray, the great books. Because she had had to make her own education, my mother valued those evenings. I was a good girl and took it all in, in part because I was one of the youngest, but I skipped first grade because my mother taught me how to read.

We all got along as siblings normally do; my older brothers teased me. Sometimes my next oldest sister wouldn't play with me. I worshipped my brother Bill; he taught me my first Latin when he came home from boarding school—I followed him around like a slave for years.

I went to college when I was sixteen; my poor roommate the first day discovered I had never been on a date. I had studied Latin from ninth through twelfth grade in high school and was prepared well in subjects such as Literature (Beowulf all the way through T.S. Eliot!), Modern and Ancient History. We had an organized and rigorous curriculum all during my Catholic schooling, taught by the Religious of the Sacred Heart; my sister Caroline Canfield Putnam became one of them and received her Doctorate at Catholic University in Philosophy. She founded the first and only school for migrant workers in America; it is still going, in the citrus groves of Indiantown, Florida, although she died in the spring of 1993 (she would have been ninety in 2012). My brothers were taught by Benedictine monks at Portsmouth Priory, and had the same rigorous Catholic education, Latin ninth through twelfth and so on.

I was an English major in college and minored in Latin; I seemed to spend half my time over at Harvard; it was right after the war 1946-50 and two of my brothers and two cousins were there. Girlfriends, sisters, cousins, tidied up and made beds on Saturday and Sunday when the biddies weren't cleaning the rooms.

In the fall of my sophomore year, the week before Thanksgiving vacation, my brother Bill who was fond of me asked if I was going to the Harvard-Yale game, and I said, "No, I have to study for a Logic exam all weekend." "You have to go," he said. "I told my friend Michael Post (your cousin's roommate) you would be coming," so what could I do—I went. We had a nice time; then I hurried home to Springfield to study for my exam. Michael went home to Danbury, Connecticut, and woke his parents at two in the morning to tell them he had met the girl he was going to marry. His mother said, "You're drunk, go to bed," but he persevered; I was only eighteen at the time. Michael's family had lived for a long time in the West, and his father, previously an English teacher, had been in the ministry at a parish in Greenwich, but was defrocked by the Episcopal Church for giving Communion to someone who was divorced. At the time, he was editor of a small paper in Connecticut called The New Milford Times; Michael's mother was a writer.

Michael was in the Class of '49 at Harvard; his brother Richard was in the Class of '51. They had an older sister named Barbara. I was a serious student and college wasn't a chore but I was quite unsure about Michael; I kept giving him up for Lent, which his friends found very amusing. Maybe that was a sign that I really liked him. And those were the days when it was assumed that after college you would get married.

When I first got to college I thought I would like to be a doctor and took Chemistry; then I realized I was never going to be able to deal with Chemistry, so I majored in English Literature; it was wonderful and writing came rather easily. Michael finished Harvard in January of '50 (his start date had been affected by the end of the War); he took a job teaching at a school called The Gunnery in Washington, Connecticut. By that time I knew I wanted to marry him.

In June of 1950, my parents took my brothers Michael and Bill and me to Europe. They had taken the older children before the War, and my oldest sister, Caroline, was making her final vows as a nun in Rome (the Mother House of the order was in Rome). The focal point was to get to Rome in the beginning of August. I spent most of my money that summer on airmail stamps writing to Michael Post; then he was drafted for the Korean War. He asked my parents for my hand when we returned in September and was told he could have it. He was sent to Fort Sam Houston in San Antonio after basic training at Fort Dix in New Jersey and learned how to be a Medic; he ended up teaching young recruits how to be a medic for a couple of years.

When he had finished his own training in February of '51, Michael called up and asked, "Which day next week would you like to be married? I have two weeks leave." We were married on February 21st in 1951 and drove off to San Antonio, Texas. Then he was transferred to Camp Pickett in Virginia, and after his two years' service he was back at his old job as teacher. I became immediately popular at The Gunnery, a boarding school, since they gave a holiday whenever a baby boy was born to a faculty wife, and two weeks after we arrived our first son was born—on September 26, 1952; we called him Michael Gregory. I had two more children at The Gunnery, but disappointed the students because both were girls.

Michael was offered a job as Dean of Boys and Head of the English Department at North Shore Country Day School in Winnetka, Illinois. We picked up lock, stock, and barrel and moved to Winnetka. The children could all go to school there because it started in kindergarten. We were in Winnetka for seven years from September of '56; Michael was also getting his Master's degree at Bread Loaf in the summertime (a program offered at Middlebury College in Vermont); we stayed with my parents in Petersham while he was at Bread Loaf (one of those summers we rented a house at Bread Loaf and were able to be all together). Then he started working toward his PhD in English at the University of Chicago.

The winter of '62-'63 Michael was diagnosed with an ulcer. He was quite tired, so we decided we would go back to Bread Loaf during the summer and each take a course rather than have him work on his PhD in Chicago. In the middle of July he was suddenly taken desperately ill with abdominal pains and rushed to the Middlebury hospital where they discovered cancer in his abdomen. He was taken by ambulance to Peter Bent Brigham in Boston; we went to stay with my parents in Petersham—I shuttled back and forth, from Michael to the five children every two days. This went on through August into September. Dr. Francis Moore, a truly lovely person, was so sweet: he suspended treatment, switching to morphine so that we could have some quality time together; Michael died in September of '63. I was with the children when he died. I went back to Boston, into the room, and he wasn't there; all I saw was a skeleton with flesh on it. In some way that body no longer had any relation to me. In a poem I wrote, "I came into the room and found a skin-covered skeleton I was afraid to kiss."

We had talked about what I should do; Michael had said I should go back and get a graduate degree and start to teach (I had done some tutoring in Latin). Because three of the children were in school (the two youngest were two and four), I took the family back to Winnetka where we stayed until late June of the next year. I applied to Northwestern and was

47

encouraged to apply to Harvard (the Dean of the Harvard Graduate School, Peter Elder, was a family friend). I applied and got in to Harvard. The house in Winnetka was on the market for quite a while; one Sunday I was invited to lunch with some school parents who knew a family anxious to move out to the suburbs. They made an offer on the house. The husband was an assistant district attorney; his wife was a teacher. The neighbors wouldn't speak to my children; Donald Rumsfeld (the Donald Rumsfeld) spoke of "inconsiderate neighbors", and I even got on television for causing such a rumpus. It was ironic too they had better jobs than most of the people on the street; they were in fact black people of consequence.

We went back East to my parents, and then I applied to the Harvard housing office. They owned several houses on Hammond Street, behind what is now the huge science building (at that time Hammond Street was behind a large parking lot). We rented the two upper floors of a two family house; I got on my bicycle every day and went over to Harvard after I had done the kids car pool. Michael went to Agassiz School, right around the corner, Barbara and Callie went to Sacred Heart Country Day with Robert Fitzgerald's wife Sally, and I took Roger and Peter to the kindergarten at Shady Hill. Someone else brought them home from Shady Hill and the girls came home in a taxi.

In 1964, when the movers were moving us in, God brought me this marvelous woman (it was a black crew and one of them asked me if I was going to need a cleaning woman). I said, "I think I'm going to need a substitute me." He said, "I think my wife would like to do that." That was Mrs. Dean; she came every day at noon and was there when the boys got home, and stayed until five so I was able to spend time at Widener Library every day after classes.

I was studying Renaissance English; my advisor told me I had to take a year of Anglo-Saxon with Professor Alfred, and I did a whole year of Chaucer with Professor Whiting. The first semester I also had Romantic Poetry with Douglas Bush and History of Literary Criticism with Walter Jackson Bate. I went to Professor Bush's office to pick up a paper at one point. He said, "I've given you an A," and he paused, "essentially I think because I don't understand what this paper is about. It's full of things about image clusters and things like that, and that's not the way I think, but I understand that some people do." I thought that was extremely generous.

In the second year I got into a seminar on the sixth book of Spenser's Faerie Queen with Walter Kaiser, and took a Marvell, Dryden, and Pope course with David Kalstone, and a mindlessly complicated course in Prosody with Craig Ladriere. There was another course—I can't remember what it was. The prerequisite for the Spenser seminar was to have read the whole Faerie Queen, but who has read the whole Faerie Queen? You read Book One because you have to for English 10 or the equivalent introductory course, and I had, but I hadn't read the rest, so I was reading The Faerie Queen practically in the shower. I left Widener one day at noon and went over to the University Restaurant and ordered whatever sandwich it was, and was reading The Faerie Queen. My sandwich came and I pushed my copy of The Faerie Queen a little to my left, and there was another copy of The Faerie Queen, and behind it was this nice man who said, "I see you're reading The Faerie Queen." Later he claimed the first thing I said was, "I'm a widow with five children." There I was, so afraid I'd like someone, and someone was going to like me and didn't know what I came with. This man looked just like James Mason at his best; he was gorgeous, very Byronic. He was writing his PhD thesis on Allegory and something else, which was why he was studying The Faerie Queen. My admission didn't seem to stop him; he started talking about his two kids, showed me their pictures which he had in his wallet. He was in the process of getting a divorce. His name was Charles Chatfield.

Charlie had been in the Naval Air Corps and started college at Bucknell, transferring to Harvard for his last two years. He went to Harvard Business School, and then he got this wonderful appointment through the State Department to work for The Marshall Plan in Paris where he lived for three years. That set him free to tell his father he was going to teach (instead of going into the family paper business). He got a job teaching at St. Mark's (a boarding school), was married (from 1956 to 1965), and here he was going for his PhD in English at Harvard. He asked me for my phone number, so I thought he would call and ask me out. I walked back to Widener Library with my Faerie Queen, and I said to myself, "He's going to ask me out to dinner." But I didn't get a call that night, and I didn't get a call the next night. The third night I did get a call: He had lost my phone number and couldn't remember my last name (he was the absent minded professor par excellence). But he did know I was in the Faerie Queen seminar, so he went over to the English Department, learned my last name and parlayed the secretary into giving him my phone number. He asked me out to dinner, and a few weeks later he asked me to a performance at the Loeb Drama Center. Very quickly we realized we loved each other.

We married after I got my MA in June of 1966 (we had met in September of 1965 and married July 30, 1966, in a house we had just bought in Belmont, Massachusetts). Charlie happily abandoned his PhD thesis so that he could teach at the Commonwealth School in Boston which was in its eighth year. It was a small school with small classes (a student teacher ratio of six to one). Everyone who taught there loved what they were doing. The kids tended to be bright, but they came from both rich and poor homes, and some of them needed a lot of help just to be at the level of their more affluent classmates (33% of the kids were, and are, on scholarship to this day, and 29% are minorities). Because it was an inner city school, there were no athletic facilities that had to be kept up, and the founder Charles Merrill (of the Merrill Lynch Merrill family), who wanted the school to be a mirror of the city population, gave a lot of his own money to the school and its endowment. Charlie taught English and was the head of the English department. He loved it; words were his life's blood.

I had already contracted to be a teaching fellow at Harvard, which I did for the next three years (During the first year I sat in a little office in Holyoke Center and saw six sophomore tutees, three junior tutees, and directed two senior theses). At the end of the first year I went to Professor Kiley who directed the freshman expository writing program and asked if I could do that. He said, "You know, that's a come down from being a teaching fellow." I said, "That doesn't matter to me—I just feel claustrophobic; I don't feel of use to enough kids." He gave me two sections of expository writing.

At the end of the third year, Charlie came home one day and said that Charles Merrill wanted me to teach at the Commonwealth School. I said, "Would you like me to teach at the Commonwealth School?" He said, "I wouldn't have brought the message if I hadn't wanted you." So we both taught at the school. I taught Latin One through Latin Five. Also, I filled in teaching English where (and when) I was needed.

Charlie was the most generous person you could possibly imagine; he really was father to all my children. Barbara, at twelve, found it hardest; she was the oldest girl and had been close to her father. Thirteen year old Michael was already showing signs of mental instability but Charlie was wonderful with him. Callie was nine and glommed onto Charlie as the father who had gone out of her life. The three oldest called him Charles—the others who had no memory of their father called him Daddy.

The Commonwealth School was unusual because of their sabbatical policy. Charlie taught an extra year so that we could go on sabbatical together; we took all the kids to Rome in 1973-1974. Out of that we developed a course back at the school called The Renaissance, a tenth grade history course. I did the history and literature and Charlie did the art history.

Eventually I took over the whole course.

In Rome we lived in an apartment. Barbara, who was majoring in Italian at Connecticut College, went to the university in Perugia for her junior year. Callie went to The Forum School, exclusively for twelfth graders, and had Italian twice a day. The younger children: Sarah, Peter, Hugh and Roger went to The New School, a spinoff of St George's (an English prep school). They all learned to speak Italian and were old enough to make the city their own. I thought I knew some Italian by the end of that year but Barbara said about me, "You think Mother is speaking Italian until you listen closely."

After the sabbatical year, we came back, this time to Maine for the summer, where we had a house Charlie had built before we were married. Charlie immediately bought nine tickets to a summer series of concerts. Old Mrs. Gribbel, in a row behind us, would feed Life Savers to the restless children (we took all of them; no one wanted to be left out). Every year, from that summer on, we bought tickets for the kids, until they were fledged. Slowly I found myself drawn into the circle that ran the series, and did things for the young quartet in residence (dinner or a musician's party, that sort of thing.) I became a member of the board, and later, somehow, I became President of Bay Chamber Concerts.

I also did things for the Episcopal Church in Camden, Maine: bake sales, the church fair, etc. In 1990 I was asked to raise money for a new church organ. I had never consciously raised money; I had written letters, but I'd never gone out and sat down with people, and asked, "Would you mind giving me ten thousand dollars?" But I said yes to the Rector, and we did raise the money: more than three hundred thousand dollars for a Schantz organ. In 1991, Sarah Rowe, who had been running something called The Community Service Project for at risk teens, asked me to join their board, and soon I was head of that organization, which later on changed its name to Youthlinks. We received a ten thousand dollar grant from The Island Institute, and used it for the down payment on a tiny house next to Oceanside, the Rockland High School.

Charlie had become Headmaster of The Commonwealth School in 1984. During the summer of 1987, Charlie's son Hugh was in a terrible car accident and suffered brain damage. Care for him filled our lives. That summer I had a grant from The National Endowment for the Humanities, to write a paper on anything I wanted, and I chose to write on Types of Simile in the Divine Comedy. I was trying to spend every minute with Hugh and write a paper at the same time. Hugh was in Spaulding, a rehab hospital for a year, and in a residential facility for another year. Then he moved to a group home, then to his own apartment in Portland, Maine.

The accident made Charlie very sad, really for the rest of his life. He retired as Headmaster in 1990 and I followed in 1991. I got much more deeply involved in raising money for Youthlinks and other volunteer organizations, and in 2002 we moved from the big house in Belmont to a townhouse in Cambridge, since Charlie had developed a blood cancer that produced too much protein in the blood.

We had gone to a specialist who discovered in Charlie a rare type of cancer called Waldenstrom's Macroglobulinemia:

blood vessels in his brain were slowly being killed off. He went into three clinical trials, and eventually each one had run its course. When that happened the blood cells swelled up, and in 2003-2004 he gradually became clinically depressed and developed dementia and exhaustion. He began to know fewer and fewer people during the winter of 2004-2005, but he recognized me to the very end when he fell into a coma and then died in March of 2005.

In the winter of 2002-2003 my brother Michael was having lunch with the general editor of a publishing project Harvard had launched called the I Tatti Renaissance Library Series (translations of Renaissance Latin poets); James Hankins was looking for translators. Michael suggested me.

I did the poems of Pietro Bembo (1470-1547); he was a Cardinal of the Catholic Church and a great patron of the arts (there is a typeface named for him). Besides translating the poetry I did an introduction and the index—it took me almost three years. It was a huge blessing for me; I could be at my desk and Charlie could be resting in his bed, and if he wanted me or needed anything, he'd just have to say Polly. The sad thing for me: the book was published after Charlie died. Most libraries order the whole series, but you can buy a single volume at the Harvard Bookstore in Cambridge.

Jim Hankins asked me to do another book, this time the poetry of Cristoforo Landino (1424-1498), a Florentine who had lived fifty years earlier than Bembo. He wrote love poems to an imaginary character and longer epistles on family incidents. Landino was a professor at what was about to become the University of Florence. That book was published in 2009. Then he gave me the Metrical Epistles of Petrarch. I translated them as best I could: they are very strange and fuzzy and difficult, with some impossible passages. I gave the impossible passages to my brother Michael and he said, "I can't make head nor tail of these." Jim said, "One or two or three fuzzy passages, but ten or twelve is just too many—I can't publish this." So there went a couple years of work.

In 2011 he gave me the poetry of Giovanni Marrasio (1400/4-1452), a Sicilian who found his way to Florence as a young man. He had a good classical education in Florence, fell in love with Angelina Piccolomini, the sister of Enea Silvio Piccolomini who became Pope Pius II. Marrasio had a manuscript of his love poems that circulated among his friends; everyone made much of him which convinced him he was on the rise. He watched as his classmates received offers of good positions, yet he didn't get anything. He went to Ferrara, to the medical school, again didn't get a job, and wrote at the end of one of his poems, "Remember to think well of men from Sicily." He wrote a number of poems for the Pope, hoping for a papal position, but when no offer came he went off to Naples where he wrote poems to King Alfonso and his courtiers. Nothing came of that. He went back home to Sicily and shortly thereafter died. I have become so fond of him because obviously his failures were just because he was a Sicilian, and the Northern Italians don't think much of Sicilians, never did. I haven't finished that book; I'm still working on it.

For translations there are two things at play, keeping in mind that the ancient language is on one page and the English is on the facing page. You don't want the Latin line five on page two to be unconnected to the English line five on page three, and I have to be close to the original text. Jim is a Professor of Renaissance History at Harvard and is fluent in Latin. Michael, a Latin scholar, is my reader, but Jim goes over everything carefully. One or the other may say, "I don't like your word there; it doesn't give the full sense of the Latin." So you have the two things at play: word/line placement and word meaning.

I've written quite a bit of my own poetry; I've had some poetry published in little magazines. It all started, I think, when we moved out to Illinois. I had some poetry published in Audience and in the Western Humanities Review; then life became busy, and overwhelming. I didn't write poetry again until I stopped teaching; I went to poetry workshops at the Cambridge Center for Adult Education. Then I started writing again.

The other part of my life, which is really, really important to me, and I never would have thought it, is being able to raise money for organizations I love, like The Maine Farmland Trust. I'm on the Capital Campaign Committee, working to preserve farmland for farming. It's a great organization. They have a program called Farmlink for farmers looking for farms, assistance with business plans, and we have actually raised 8.9 million of a 10 million dollar campaign. We received a million dollar gift from an individual, and a million and a half from a foundation. When we raise the 10 million, that will leverage money from federal and state agencies: 50 million dollars to preserve 100,000 acres of farmland, an annuity for the State of

Maine. We've already preserved 35,000 acres on our own. Maine used to be the breadbasket of New England; it can be again.

I feel my efforts count, with all the organizations I have joined, even a cemetery committee, and an Episcopal monastery in Cambridge. The Brothers at the monastery have been good to me, and were good to my first husband when he was at Harvard (he served there as an acolyte), and when he died, they were there to help. The man who runs The Friends of St. John the Evangelist Monastery spotted me and asked if I would help with fund raising for the restoration of the monastery. So it goes.

The genes in this family are something else: In 2012 I turned eighty-three. My oldest brother Roger was ninety and the oldest licensed flying instructor in the country; he lives in Wellfleet on the Cape. My brother Bill, for years President of the American Alpine Club, lost a lung during the war so he can't climb over 10,000 feet, but he did all the mapping of the Selkirk Range in British Columbia, and in 2012 at eighty-eight, is sole trustee of the Lowell Observatory. My sister Anna, eighty-six, is a genealogist and artist who took the earliest records of the Town of Chatham, which were practically indecipherable, and put them into modern English. She recently wrote and illustrated three books featuring her cat Lucius, to raise money for the animal shelter on Martha's Vineyard where she lives. Michael, the youngest at 79, was recently elected a Life Trustee at the American Academy in Rome, one of only two so honored. He is the W. Duncan Professor of Classics and Comparative Literature Emeritus at

Brown University and continues as a leading Virgil scholar who hasn't stopped writing his wonderful books (16 at last count!). Our eldest sister is dead, but the rest of us haven't slowed down, not a bit.

Douglas Vincent O'Dell, Junior

Major General Marine Corps (Ret), father of five sons, Partner AIM Investments (Ret)

About 25 or 30 years ago, my brother was rummaging around the Vermont Historical Society library in Montpelier and came across a book that had been written in 1932 called The History of the O'Dell Family in North America, written by a woman named Wilson whose maiden name had been O'Dell; she was from the Wisconsin branch of the family and enjoyed an advantage of time and place: there were older relatives still living who could reach back into the 19th century and tell her where her O'Dell forebears came from. Coupling that information with some pretty thorough research, I discovered that our ancestors came from England to the Massachusetts Bay Colony in 1636. Apparently they chafed under Puritan rigidity and ended up in Norwalk, Connecticut, as merchants, farmers, and mechanics (the general term for harness makers, blacksmiths, carpenters, etc.)

At the time of the American Revolution Joseph O'Dell was living in the upper Hudson River Valley with his family: a wife, six sons and several daughters (the O'Dell's were still farmers and mechanics). Joseph and his sons served in the Continental Army as enlisted men, participating in the battles of Saratoga, the retreat from Long Island and White Plains, and other campaigns. Joseph had the rank of sergeant, and in order to get troops to re-enlist after nine to twelve months service, the legislatures of the various colonies had to come up with inducements to raise regiments. New York came up with the promise of land grants in the upper Hudson River and Mohawk River Valleys.

When the war was at an end, land speculation resulted in the New York Legislature reneging on the land grants, which ended up in the hands of the legislators friends. Joseph O'Dell, exhibiting what I like to think of as the stiff-necked individualism of the O'Dell family, picked up and moved to the eastern townships of Quebec with his whole family, to take advantage of land grants being offered by the Canadians. That was in the 1790's. They moved to a place that today is actually called O'Dellville. Joseph became a successful merchant with agricultural holdings and died in 1819, apparently leaving a fairly sizable estate, the division of which caused a schism in the family. As a result, half a large family moved to the territory which is now Wisconsin. My direct lineage remained in O'Dellville, and that is where my great great grandfather Silas O'Dell was born; his son, George O'Dell, re-emigrated to the U.S. around 1880, and became a citizen in 1882 of Moriah, New York (I have a copy of his citizenship certificate issued in Port Henry, a community close to Moriah on the New York side of Lake Champlain).

George O'Dell was a talented pattern-maker and settled in New York State to work in a foundry, married Mary Murphy and ultimately had nine children, the sixth of whom was my grandfather Wilburt Francis O'Dell, born in Moriah in1892. Shortly after Wilburt's birth, George and a friend came to Pottstown, Pennsylvania, an iron and steel center, and got work at the Great Eastern Steel Foundry on the Schuylkill River. Six months later, his wife (with six children) came to

Pottstown on a series of canal barges, and ended up in a house that was referred to as 'half a double'. We have always been proud of the fact that the only black family in Pottstown, the Butlers, had the other half of that house. We were among the few Catholics and they were the only African Americans. The two families remain close to this day.

My great grandfather was one of the founding members of the Catholic parish in Pottstown: Saint Aloysius, where my grandfather went to school through the eighth grade. At the age of thirteen my grandfather went to work in the foundries 'cutting sand' (an entry level job where young boys would shovel sand through a series of finer and finer screens to make the sand fine enough to mold iron and steel patterns). Wib as he was called worked in the foundry business from 1905 until he retired in 1968. He had married Caroline Estelle Koechel, the 5th child of a Chester County German immigrant farming family that had been in northern Chester County since the 1850s. They were Lutherans who had been assimilated into the wider Montgomery-Berks-Chester County English speaking community early on (English Quakers were in the majority in Pottstown and had started the foundry business).

My grandmother was just a year younger than my grandfather, who, in addition to his foundry job, had a part time job delivering for a ladies millinery shop in Pottstown called Ellis Mills (he was seventeen). The story goes that one day he was asked to deliver a hat to the residence of Thomas Koechel, and when he did, Thomas Koechel's daughter Caroline answered the door. In short order they became a pair and were married in April of 1912. My uncle, Wilburt F.

O'Dell, Jr., arrived in October of 1912. Up to the time my grandfather died, no one in my generation had ever quite made the connection between the wedding and birth dates, until we were at graveside and my brother recalled the priest reciting the wedding date of my grandparents. My brother looked at my uncle's headstone and blurted out, "Wait a minute—that's only six months!" (My grandfather had outlived both my father and my uncle).

Further research revealed that Thomas Koechel was not happy about his daughter's predicament in early 1912. He had a livery stable and was also a successful businessman and town burgher; he essentially disowned my grandmother, first, because of the situation, and second, because she proceeded to marry a Catholic (he was a devout Lutheran). When my grandfather went to rent a carriage to take them to the train station for their wedding trip to Reading (all of about fifteen miles away), he rented from my great grandfather Koechel's competitor.

By the time he retired Wib O'Dell was Vice President and General Manager of March-Brownback Iron Foundry in Pottstown. They were what is called a gray iron foundry and manufactured agricultural tools, Franklin stoves (where they got their start), more ornate stoves as time went on, and consumer products like the heavy umbrella stands for picnic tables; they even made limited quantities of the harder ware iron for rail car brake shoes. The gray iron was inexpensive to make and was perfect for stoves as it heated up quickly and retained heat, though it could be brittle in thin castings and was not as pure as ware iron or malleable iron (a more flexible iron). Gray iron also machined easily. For 19th and 20th century consumer products it was the preferred kind of iron.

I learned a lot about iron in conversations with my grandfather; we were very close, and I worked briefly in a malleable iron foundry in Easton, Pennsylvania in 1974. My grandfather used to have nightmares about me losing fingers and limbs when I worked there; he lived to be almost ninety-seven; his mind was sharp and he had a vise grip of a handshake to the very end. As tough a guy as he was, my grandfather was one of the most gentle men I have ever known; he never drove a car though he owned cars (bought for his sons). For most of his life he lived at 521 North Charlotte Street in Pottstown, a two mile walk to the foundry. He would walk to the foundry in the morning, walk home at lunch, walk back after lunch and walk home at night; he flew for the first time when he was in his eighties.

Back in 1912, upon their return from Reading, my grandfather and my grandmother started out in modest circumstances; he went back to work at the foundry. My grandmother continued to attend the Lutheran church prior to joining my grandfather at Catholic services (later his son, my father sang in the Lutheran church choir while at the same time serving as an altar boy in the Catholic church; my grandmother ultimately converted to the Catholic church around 1957). As I've already said, my uncle Wilburt came along in October of 1912; then came my father Douglas in October of 1914 and my uncle Jim in 1917. Aunt Betty arrived in 1918 (she just died last year, the last of the siblings to die).

My grandmother was the original iron lady; she could be stern, especially with her daughters-in-law. She was a proud woman: in 1979 in her eighties she broke her hip and had surgery. My father and his siblings thought it best if their parents were moved into assisted living. My grandmother had proudly told her friends, "My children would never put me in a home." They put her in a home on a Saturday; on Sunday when the whole family visited she was lying in bed rigid as a board, barely speaking, obviously angry and heartbroken—she was dead by Tuesday morning. My grandfather moved in with my aunt, his daughter, and lived another ten years. It may have been a sort of liberating experience for him. He travelled, to California to visit my cousin, and he went other places.

In 1989, when he was ninety six he felt some sort of discomfort. They put him in the hospital for testing (it was the first time he had been in a hospital in his entire life). My uncle, who by that time was his sole surviving son, came and had breakfast with him in the hospital at eight or nine in the morning. My grandfather said, "You know, I'm going to take a nap." He went to sleep and never woke up. Wilburt Francis O'Dell had a wonderful, wonderful life; that was the way to go.

My father, Douglas Vincent O'Dell, born in 1914, was a precocious little fellow who did extremely well at Saint Aloysius through the eighth grade and then Pottstown High School. He skipped a couple grades and graduated at just sixteen. He was a talented cornet player who started playing with bands at local speakeasy's when he was thirteen or fourteen to make ends meet (at that time his father was only a shop foreman).

He applied and was accepted at Ursinus College and did well academically, but we're now talking about the depths of the Great Depression (he started college in the fall of 1931). In 1934-35, to help keep the family afloat and save some money for his last year at college, he took a job as a riveter's assistant at the Carpenter Steel Plant in Reading, Pennsylvania. A red hot rivet would be thrown up to him, out of the fire; he caught it in something that looked like a funnel with a handle and grabbed onto it with a pair of tongs. He put the rivet in a bored hole between two steel plates for the waiting riveter, who riveted the hot, soft, back side of the rivet (looking like a short, fat nail) from the opposite side with an air hammer, connecting steel beams; the rivet expanded and hardened when it cooled. My father did that for about a year, went back to college and graduated, class of 1936, majoring in English. His first job out of college was selling vacuum cleaners door to door.

My grandparents were both Democrats in a town that was deeply Republican and had been forever. However, my great grandfather was a leader in the Republican Party. Some of the leaders of the Republican Party came to my grandfather and asked him to switch parties, being a well-respected leader at his work, to help in the 1936 elections. As an inducement, they offered my father a job teaching English at Pottstown High School. My grandparents switched their political affiliation and my father stopped selling vacuum cleaners, although my grandparents continued to vote Democratic.

He taught English for three years and in 1939-1940 enlisted in the Army Air Corps as an Air Cadet, knowing realistically that war was coming, but he was not successful in the Air Corps (he told me he used to bounce the bi-plane trainers landing them); he was returned to the Army reserves. The Army called him back after Pearl Harbor and sent him to Officers Candidate School. In the late spring of 1942 he embarked for the Aleutians Campaign. The westernmost Aleutians, Kiska and Attu, were part of the Alaska Territory and had been captured and occupied by the Japanese. It was a cold and miserable campaign—amphibious operations in the extreme cold are never fun (I've done them); he was in the second island assault. Ultimately successful, but later was known as 'the forgotten campaign,' it was overshadowed by Guadalcanal. My father was an infantry officer, 5'7", 135 lbs soaking wet. His outfit was comprised of Missouri National Guard troops who had been called up; he was the only non-Missourian. Although a 2nd lieutenant, he was a company commander (he spent sixteen months there).

In the Aleutians my father came across a large, deep red spaniel, a puppy that was part cocker; he adopted him and named him Smoky. You couldn't bring a dog back to the States, but one of his sergeants slipped the dog a hot dog with a few sleeping pills and put him in a gunny sack; they took a ship from Dutch Harbor back to Prince Rupert on the Canadian shore, and then a train from Prince Rupert all the way down to Missouri, arriving in the early summer (the train was air conditioned and went through the beautiful Canadian Rockies). The dog did not take well to the hot climate in Missouri, having come from the Aleutians, so the troops dug him a pit which they filled with 18 inches of water so that Smoky could stay cool. He eventually came to Pottstown and stayed with my grandparents when my father was assigned to the 106th Infantry Division during the fall of 1943. He joined the 106th at Camp Atterbury in Indiana, just south of Indianapolis, as a first lieutenant attached to Company K, 3rd Battalion, 422nd Infantry.

It was late in the war, filled almost completely with National Guard troops and conscripts. Very few people in the Division had any combat experience; my father was the only officer in his company who had been deployed previously. His company commander Hank Harmeling came from an Army Family, graduated West Point class of '42, AGR (accelerated graduation rate), and was much younger than my father who was 29, a real good guy. He went from 2nd lieutenant to Captain in no time flat; my father thought the world of him.

They went to England in August of 1944 on the Aquitania, a sister ship of the Lusitania. The officers were eating high off the hog in what would otherwise have been first class while the troops were getting short rations. The officers would sneak food from the first class mess down to the troops. They ended up in Stow-on-the-Wold (in the Cotswolds) for further training, and then were deployed to France in November of '44, where they were trucked to the front (my father celebrated his birthday en route).

The 106th Division was replacing the 2nd Infantry Division, which had been in the field since D-Day advancing right up to the German Belgium border at the Schnee Eifel, an ancient, heavily forested 2000 foot mountain ridge that defines the border, the spine of which was part of the Siegfried Line filled with heavily armed bunkers built by the Germans between the wars to defend the border. When my father's units got up there they were actually in Germany by a couple of hundred meters and moved into the bunkers, which meant they were faced into Germany.

The Schnee Eifel is cut by a series of fairly steep vails reminiscent of the Blue Mountains of Pennsylvania; east and west of them are open plains, good defensive terrain but not ideal for offense. The only place for military movement was the Losheim Gap, which the Germans planned to take; they would converge on Bastogne on their way to the Port of Antwerp. My father's 122nd Regiment was on the northern end at the top of the Schnee Eifel facing third grade German forces (the crack German forces had been withdrawn in preparation for the main offensive). There were a few patrols and some minor exchanges of fire, prisoners taken (my father was a weapons platoon commander: mortars, anti-tank rockets, etc.).

Saint Vith, a Belgian town 16 miles to the rear of the forward edge of the battle area, was where the 106th Division headquarters were located and they were under attack. They had no way of knowing the Battle of the Bulge was underway; that's how quickly the Germans encircled the Division. The 424th Regiment of the 106th, which was at the southern end of the Gap, managed to get out relatively intact, the 422nd and 423rd (my father being in the 422nd), tried to fight their way out and got hung up on the Our river that finds the back side of the Schnee Eifel in a place called Schoenberg. The Germans had already captured the crossing, and a road that runs parallel to the river on the west side of the Schnee Eifel was choked with German military traffic. My father and his units got down to Schoenberg and into a brief fire fight, but it was obvious they were in a hopeless situation, having expended most of their ammunition and food against a mechanized force, with 20 inches of snow on the ground.

The regimental commander on the spot elected to surrender. My father and all his mates, 3000-3500, were taken prisoner on the 20th of December 1944 and were stripped of everything; a portion of the 423rd were also taken which brought the total count to around 6000. The officers were separated from their men; Christmas Eve 1944 my father spent in a locked up railroad car that was so crowded they had to take turns standing and sitting down. The inside of the car was coated with ice, and to make matters worse, the British were bombing the railroad yard.

Shortly thereafter they ended up in a place called Hammelburg, in a POW camp that had been the German Army Infantry School; it was a small place, but due to the ensuing events there were 2500 Allied prisoners: British, American, Serbians from the Russian army, and in January a large group of American prisoners marched from Poland (they had been held in a German Oflag, or prison, having originally been captured in North Africa in 1942). Among them was George Patton's son in law John Waters, a lieutenant colonel at the time. As of February 1st, 1945, they were all still cramped into quarters built for 600.

My father, who spoke German, and was pretty small and nimble, shuttled at night from the US camp to the Serbian camp to barter for Red Cross supplies that were ending up with the Serbians (things like cigarettes and coffee); we have pictures of him in these huts. He used to get letters from guys in Serbia when I was a boy.

In late March, early April, Patton learned that his son in

law was in the prison camp (by that time the American front was 60 miles from Hammelburg). He decided that he was going to launch a raid to liberate the POW camp behind German lines, led by Max Baum (there are multiple books written on Task Force Baum, including the historian John Toland's Last Hundred Days—my father is mentioned). Max was still alive in 2012, living in California—I have met him: a burly Jewish fellow from New York who had been in the rag trade (he turned out to be one of Patton's young, more aggressive Armor officers).

Task Force Baum went charging behind the German lines, had early success, but as luck would have it, there was an anti-tank unit resting at the camp. They got into a fire fight—there are pictures of the Sherman tanks coming through the wire. In the ensuing melee my father and a couple of other guys headed out over the countryside, but it was clear this was not going to work (John Waters was shot at close range in the stomach by a German high powered rifle, but survived ultimately to become a lieutenant general!).

My father was recaptured and several days later, leaving remnants of the camp behind (some wounded like John Waters), the remaining prisoners of war, including my father, were marched into southeastern Germany toward Nuremberg in advance of the Allied forces. They showed up at the German rail yard at Furth (not far from Nuremberg) at about noon around the 17th of April, the supposition (pure speculation) being that the Germans would hold the prisoners for ransom pending some final settlement of the War (Hitler was still alive at the time, until the 2nd of May).

Sitting at the railroad yard waiting for train transportation,

71

there was an American air raid—my father lost his leg below the left knee (that part of the story told by the Chaplain in John Toland's book). Ironically, he had been promoted to Captain but didn't know it. The rest of the troops were marched off, some scurrying into the countryside (his company commander, Hank Harmeling, was one who escaped). My father was moved to a German field hospital in a bombed out school building, and a British Army major, with a Serbian doctor, took off what was left of his leg with a kitchen knife and no anesthetic; otherwise he would have bled to death. Two days later the Americans arrived; the first guy in the door was from Phoenixville, Pennsylvania, just a few miles down the road from where my father was raised. The second guy in the door was his squad leader, a classmate of my father.

My father now got the deluxe treatment; they loaded him into an ambulance along with other American wounded they had recovered, and started in the direction of Wiesbaden, a major airhead, with the intention of evacuating him to a triage hospital. On the way, at a refueling stop, they ran across a group of GI's who had recently liberated a cache of French champagne that had been appropriated by the Wehrmacht. Over the French label were these stampings, "Property of the Wehrmacht—Not to be drunk." They gave my father 5 bottles of champagne, 2 of which he consumed immediately. At Wiesbaden, he was put on a hospital plane (John Waters was on the same plane). They flew back to the States and landed at Presque Isle, Maine, where my father called my grandmother, the first communication from him since before he was captured. My grandmother fainted; she had been having recurrent nightmares that my father was blinded. When she recovered he said, "I've lost my leg." She responded, "That's ok." He proceeded to Walter Reed Hospital where he had multiple surgeries and spent 16 months learning to walk with his prosthesis, with some trips home.

By the fall of 1946 he was regularly spending time at home, and was sort of the local hometown hero. He met a recently discharged Navy nurse from Reading, Pennsylvania, Ann Noll, who he had known briefly when she was a nursing student before the war, the middle child of 12. They began to date, and my father, who was not getting any younger at 32, asked her to marry him; she accepted, and they were married on May 10th, 1947. I came along May 30th, 1948.

My father decided he was not going to return to a career in education. The local Chevy-Oldsmobile dealer had a car with an automatic transmission on display; Mr. Kaiser, the owner, got permission from General Motors to sell the car to my father so my father could drive. It was the first car with an automatic transmission in the town.

He decided to start in the real estate business, and got himself hired by Jim Moore, an established real estate broker. The town of Pottstown had coalesced around my father, and ironically, a lot of the kids he had taught in high school were now returning G.I.'s. Here was their high school teacher who had lost a leg, fought in two theaters: in the Pacific and Europe; they trusted him.

When I was two or three months old, my parents put me in a laundry basket to go out to a farm owned by Jim Moore. My mother came out and found a mouse running up and down the basket with me in it. My mother did not deal well with

73

rodents of any size. In fairly short order, fifteen months, my brother Tim was born and then my sister, three years younger; she was born on my father's birthday, October 19th. We had one other brother, Chris, born in July of '56; he died at the age of 17 of an atrial aneurysm in '73. In 2012 my mother was 91, still living in Pottstown on her own: still drinks, still smokes, has a convertible. My sister lives in the house I was raised in; my brother lives in Vermont. My father, as I have reflected, died of his wounds on December 13th, 1985: diabetes, cancer, you name it.

In the postwar era, in Pottstown, we didn't have a huge house, but it was a custom built house, architect designed for my father's needs (first floor bedroom, which in those days was a little unusual). My father, as I like to describe him, was a warrior-poet. He loved language and was a voracious reader, a huge fan of Shakespeare; he loved the turn of English phrases and puns. One of his favorite expressions was, "This meal was an elegant sufficiency; anything more would be a superfluity." He loved the meter of language and speech, language both written and spoken. He reveled in the small ironies of life and his view of the world was Horatio Alger-esque. As a boy, he had the gift of virtue, growing up in a fairly protected environment, not that he didn't work hard or was given any extraordinary privileges.

My father was a breakout guy, the first O'Dell to go to college, and my mother came from similar means, a large German-Irish family in Reading. Her father ran concessions in the knitting mills: newspapers, candy, that kind of stuff, probably 'made book' on the side. He was an active volunteer fireman in Reading; my cousins on that side are all firemen to this day! But my mother went to nursing school in Pottstown (in those days you received a Certificate). After she did her stint in the Navy at 26 (when she was dating my father after the war), she got her Bachelor's at Penn; train service to Philadelphia was only 45 minutes.

Among the shaping influences in my life were my family and the small town values that surrounded me. My mother was the disciplinarian in our family; she could be pretty tough. My father was gentle with us, although he left Jim Moore and started his own successful real estate agency. He brought in his brother who sold life insurance; they became the O'Dell Agency for Real Estate, Property and Casualty Insurance. It was a good move; he would sell a house then issue the insurance policy. There were all those thousand square foot starter houses, small Cape Cods, 2nd floors often unfinished, which allowed a new homeowner to decide what he was going to do with the two bedrooms on the first floor. They were sprouting up like mushrooms around Pottstown—functional, better built than what you can get today—they still survive. Then of course there were still more returning GI's who needed a roof over their heads, many of them his former students.

My father went into partnership with several builders, one of them Bobby Gresh, who was considerably younger; they bought land, sometimes together with silent partners, and went through the subdivision process—Bobby would build the houses, my father would sell them. They did four or five serious subdivisions in the 50s and 60s; when I was 16 and 17, I worked two summers for Bobby, hammering nails. His foreman was a highly skilled Pennsylvania-German carpenter, Elmer Heimbach, a wonderful guy; I learned a lot from him.

The country club in Pottstown started just after the First World War; my grandfather was not a golfer, but he was an early member. Before he went to war, my father was an avid golfer and outdoorsman; he was in an informal group of raconteurs during the late 30s, including guys that played cards late into the night: my father was an expert card player. In the postwar years, after losing a leg, his only mano a mano outlet was playing cards. Every Saturday and Sunday afternoon his routine was to play gin rummy; he played poker on Monday nights, a tradition that had started when he was in his twenties. He played with Bob Smith, the founder of Mrs. Smith's pies, Abe Pollack, the scion of Pollack Steel (which still exists in Pottstown), the Joneses of Jones Trucking; these were men of extraordinary wealth in some cases. I'm talking about the 50s and 60s when the pots on the table were six and seven thousand dollars! My father had a steel trap, mathematical mind, which I do not (I don't enjoy playing cards—I think it skips a generation). I have a nephew, my brother's son, who is a very good card player; he's in a PhD Math program at Durham University in England. He makes a couple thousand dollars a week playing poker.

In his later years he walked with a cane, but even though he walked without a limp earlier, he never played golf or went fishing after coming back from the war. In cold and damp weather he felt the pain. I learned from birth about the problems with prosthetics, the issues that had to be faced later in life. For instance, one prosthetic did not last a lifetime, and it had to be continually re-fit; it has gotten worlds better since my father's generation.

My father was on the Pottstown School Board starting in 1960; he knew what was and what was not going on in the Pottstown schools. There was a new Catholic high school, St. Pius, in Pottstown that was ok. It was where all my cousins ended up going to school for the most part. I went to St. Aloysius through 8th grade; all my friends were going on to St. Pius. My mother got it into her mind that she wanted me to be Jesuit educated at St. Joseph's Prep in South Philadelphia. I could commute by train leaving Pottstown at 6:30am, followed by a bus and a trolley in Philadelphia, arriving at school at 8:15am, then repeating the commute after school back to Pottstown.

My mother and father brought me down to St. Joe's in 1962; they met with a priest while I sat in an anteroom waiting. The practical Jesuit apparently said, "Let me get this straight—You want him commuting three hours at the age of 14 to get a Jesuit education, when, a half mile from where you live, is one of the best schools in the world, The Hill School?" My mother was taken aback; my father smirked on the side, having been an educator, and been on the school board. Also, he knew many men on The Hill School faculty, as the country club was, in effect, their faculty club (50% of the club grounds were and still are owned by the school). The core of the building that represents the club house was the barracks for The Hill School ROTC in the First World War. The faculty dined there on a regular basis and the trustees met there. A lot of my parents friends after they were married, social contemporaries and war veterans, were either pre-war, or new

77

young members of The Hill School faculty, like the Moffett family (Jim was Associate Headmaster and Director of Admissions).

I applied to The Hill School and went to take a battery of tests; I tested ok, above my grades, which is the story of my life (an under-achiever). I was accepted in the 8th grade (from 8th grade at St. Aloysius to 8th grade at The Hill School, which was still a 2 year quantum leap). I was 14 and had just turned 19 when I graduated.

My five years at the school, not so much in the classroom, but on the playing fields and in the dormitories, and, I guess, to some degree in the chapel, were the second shaping influence in my life. I was a day boy four of the five years (there was a requirement for day students: you had to board for at least one year). I would have preferred to board all five years, because when you go to a boarding school as a day student, you miss about 40% of the experience. Home was a 15 minute walk from the campus, a little over a mile. In the years when I was a day student, my father would drop us off—my brother followed me by a year, and we walked home at night.

The Hill School is a much different place today than it was then; I think it's a better place today. It was all boys, very regimented, stuck in the twenties in some respects, heavy in the humanities (which was a good thing). I was an ambivalent student, especially when it came to the sciences, and I struggled mightily with math. I was a good athlete, started on the varsity football team at halfback, and played ice hockey. I injured my right knee senior year playing football. I ran track, but couldn't do that my 6th Form year due to the injury (the knee was successfully operated on pretty invasively a couple days after graduation). I played football, ice hockey, and rugby all through college at Rutgers, and then spent four years in the infantry.

I did not get very good college advice at Hill, which, looking back, I regret. I applied to three schools: George Washington, Boston College and Rutgers and was accepted at all three, which may mean I undershot the mark. I probably should have stretched for some place like Brown, or maybe even Cornell. I might have been good enough to play varsity football at a place like Bucknell, or even at Rutgers, where I played lightweight football, but I had more fun playing rugby anyway.

The coaching at The Hill School was a whole lot better than what I got at Rutgers. In hindsight I should have gone to a Division II or Division III school, something like a Dickinson. Remember, I was going from a class size of ten, to a class size of 250 with a teaching assistant at the head of the class droning on about the Peloponnesian War, which I had studied in depth at Hill in 9th or 10th grade (I should have saved the papers I wrote). It was just not a satisfactory academic experience. It wasn't until junior and senior year at Rutgers, when I was in seminars with six, eight, ten students, dealing with department heads and other tenured professors, asking serious questions, that things got better. I arrived in 1967 to all the campus unrest (the Tet Offensive was during the spring term)—that didn't help. But I don't want to come down too hard on Rutgers; at The Hill School I was in a privileged environment, where many of the students came from multi-generational Hill School families with money, whereas Rutgers was filled with first generation blue collar Newark, North Jersey kids from across the ethnic spectrum; it was a positive eye opener.

I enlisted in the Marine Corps in March of 1968, having started that process in the fall of 1967. The Marine Corps by itself does not have an ROTC. It shares in the Naval ROTC program, but there was no Naval ROTC at Rutgers, never had been. I was pretty certain I didn't want to be an Army officer, but all decisions at that time were influenced by the draft, a shadow hovering; you could be drafted at any time, so you needed to have some wisdom afoot and begin to shape what your life was going to be after college.

I enlisted in the Marine Corps Platoon Leaders Class Program, a program exclusive to the Marine Corps that dates from a few years before World War II. You enlist as a private with no explicit responsibilities during the school year, but with two six week duty increments spread over two summers at Quantico during college, or one ten week increment. I did my first increment after my freshman year in 1968, and went back for my second increment after my junior year in 1970. The Selection Officer came to visit in the interim, to make sure you maintained your physical fitness, and to get help in recruiting other kids on campus.

During my second increment in the summer of 1970 I reinjured my knee four weeks into the six week program. I was sent home NPQ (Not Physically Qualified). I was later readmitted to the program, and two days after graduation was back at Quantico for a third six week increment. I completed that and was commissioned on July 16th, 1971 as a second lieutenant. I had received neither scholarship money nor a stipend during my four years at Rutgers, like the students enrolled in the Army ROTC program. But at that time Rutgers was around $5000 a year, Trinity $10,000, where my brother went to college, and Manhattanville, $8500, my sister's college. It was a bargain, even for someone from out of state going to a state school.

I immediately went on active duty as an infantry officer, went to The Basic School at Quantico, and at that time met the first Mrs. O'Dell, Eileen Kiminer (Dr. Freud would intervene here and say "I think you married your mother!"). Her father was a retired Navy captain; we were married in August of 1972. I was stationed on the West Coast (the First Marine Division). Our oldest son was born in August of 1973 in San Clemente, California: Douglas V. O'Dell III. With great ambivalence I left active duty in 1974 after my brother died. I felt I needed to come home to Pennsylvania to hold the family together (my father was in tough shape). I left the Marine Corps as a Senior First Lieutenant and was promoted to Captain later that year in the Reserves.

One of the realities in those days in the Marine Corps, after an initial tour in the States, would be deployment for a year in Okinawa, which was not an appealing prospect. The immediate post-Vietnam Marine Corps in the seventies was a mixed bag: we had incipient drug, alcohol, and racial issues; discipline was in rough shape. I think we were starting to turn the corner, but senior leadership in many cases was in denial—they thought they were still dealing with the Marine Corps of 1946. Change was needed, but I made a conscious decision to stay in the reserves, as I tried my hand at civilian life.

My first job, the job I was able to get (this was in 1974 when the Economy was on its knees), was as a foreman in a foundry in Easton, Pennsylvania. We rented a little stone farmhouse up on the Bushkill Creek north of Easton. I got hired away from there to go to work for Ingersoll Rand in their pump and condenser plant as a purchasing agent in Allentown, Pennsylvania. We moved into slightly more ideal quarters, an apartment complex, and our second son, Andy, was born in July of 1975, just after we moved. Because my wife had been pregnant before I started working for Ingersoll Rand, we were not covered with insurance.

My father in law had given us two shares of IBM stock as a gift (it was worth around $150 a share). When Andy was born I needed to sell those shares to bail him out of the hospital. In the course of selling, at the Merrill Lynch office in Allentown, I met the manager: Jack McNary, who essentially offered me a job, also in July of 1975; I ended up going to work at Merrill Lynch in October. That began my work in the financial services business, parallel to my career in the Marine Corps Reserves.

I was a brand new Captain and the Executive Officer of Headquarters Company, 4th Service Battalion, in Bethlehem, Pennsylvania. In those days it was the more conventional one weekend a month, maybe a couple of hours in between, and 2 weeks in the summer. That doesn't exist anymore and hasn't for decades, the 'weekend warrior' kind of thing. I was part of the post-Vietnam Marine Corps generation; all my first lieutenants and the captains I worked with, had at least one tour in Vietnam. I did not, which is probably just as well.

I knew that the training we were giving our enlisted troops was not adequate even to peacetime needs: the safe discharge of firearms, how to maintain weapons and equipment (even communications equipment). I made it my pledge that I was going to do what I could to make the Marine Corps Reserve, specifically the 4th Marine Corps Division, relevant to the needs of the Marine Corps writ large, in the last quarter of the 20th Century, even if we never were activated. In the event we were activated, I wanted to be sure we could be full and contributing partners with the total force and in the nation's defense. That required some study, some rigor; it required me to be sort of outside the mainstream relative to my peers, many of whom were there just because it was an extra paycheck, or it was their 'guys weekend off.' It's not that I didn't enjoy a 'hail fellow well met' atmosphere. I was convinced there was going to be a time when the needs of the Marine Corps were going to include the activation of all or part of the Reserves to confront threats to the nation. I held that point of view right up to Desert Storm when a good part of the Reserve was activated.

I returned to the infantry: 2nd Battalion 25th Marines, in 1977. Headquarters were in Garden City, Long Island, with subordinate infantry companies spread all over New Jersey and in one case Harrisburg, Pennsylvania, which was the reserve unit I joined (they were looking for an infantry officer and I was looking for an infantry unit—I was still a Captain). Eileen and I had two sons by that time: Douglas III and Andy, and my marriage was beginning to unwind. We had separated a couple of times, and separated for good in the fall of 1980. She ultimately moved back to Arlington, Virginia, where her family lived. I had left Merrill Lynch and gone to Kidder Peabody in Reading, Pennsylvania, but moved to New York in 1980, and started working for L.F. Rothschild (I actually worked for an affiliate of Rothschild called Minoco, a unit developing oil and gas opportunities all over the U.S. and overseas). I was one of the people looking to raise highly incented capital (during the late 70s and early 80s the country was awash with tax incented deals).

I lived in Manhattan and one weekend a month I travelled to Garden City; I was the Fire Support Coordinator for the battalion, which meant that I worked in the operations section coordinating all the indirect fires: artillery, mortars, and air (integration of fires and maneuver is a hallmark of the Marine Corps, different from the way the Army does it). Living in New York as a single 31 year old guy in an apartment on the upper East Side, you might just as well have been in prison on Rikers Island. You came home to a dark apartment—you woke up in an empty apartment.

Minoco began winding down operations in late 1981-82; at the same time I was offered a job with the Bank of New Jersey in Southern New Jersey as a Vice President of Corporate Finance. I moved to a little farmhouse in Chester County, Pennsylvania, which I proceeded to restore after work, hammering nails, plastering, etc. In the course of the summer of 1982 an old acquaintance of mine called me up and said, "There's a woman I'd like you to meet." I knew of Judy Pizzica (her previous married name), having met her once a few years earlier; she was a CPA living in Ardmore, Pennsylvania, in a big, drafty, old Victorian house with three little boys.

They were at the time seven, five, and four, and she was in the process of getting a divorce. My friend, who had been a college friend of Judy's, got us together at a backyard cookout in Wynnewood Pennsylvania on August 13, a Friday, in 1982. We had a pleasant time together; she was going to the Jersey shore the next day with her three children for a week. I drove down and met her for dinner; the following weekend I went to Eastern Long Island where I was sharing a group house in Sag Harbor, but the weather was bad, so I called her up and said, "Hey, I'm going to come back to Pennsylvania—do you want to go out for dinner on Sunday night?" She said yes and the next day she said. "Do you want to come over to my house for dinner?" I said, "Sure." We were sitting in her backyard cooking steaks, drinking wine. I proposed; she accepted. That was it, ten days into the relationship; going on 31 years in 2012.

The overlap in our sons made it even more natural; the boys are closer than many biological brothers. It's mine, hers, mine, hers, hers, and they're all within five years in age. My boys were not living with me, but especially after Judy and I married, the five guys would end up spending the better part of four to five weeks a year together. My philosophy as a divorced father was that I had to depend on my long term relationship with my sons, and as long as I remained in contact with them, and was a real presence in their lives, that was what counted. I had witnessed civil wars in other divorced parents where the children were the ultimate victims. My first wife remarried twice; her second marriage was terrible, and her third was to a fellow who was considerably older. He died in September of 2005, and she died in November of 2008.

Both of my sons had, to one degree or another, some minor learning disabilities: my son Trip (Douglas III) ended up graduating from Gonzaga College High School, which is the Jesuit high school in Washington. He accepted and learned to live with his disabilities, and went on to Xavier University in Ohio; in 2003 he received a Master's Degree in Multimedia from Indiana University, which at that time was a new field; he went on to work in Silicon Valley until recently when he and his family moved back east to Montclair.

Andy followed Trip at Gonzaga, but did not accept his learning disabilities; he capitalized on the fact that he was a cute little boy, athletically gifted, and charmed his way through a lot of situations, but also became a disciplinary problem (he and his mother were oil and water); he did not finish at Gonzaga, but did finish at Archbishop O'Connell, the local Catholic high school in northern Virginia, and began a six year odyssey in various colleges, finally graduating from Wynn University in Florida. Andy, who could sell ice to Eskimos, is one of those kids who has to touch a burning candle twice to make sure it's hot. He had some false starts, including a marriage that only lasted around eighteen months (not because of him). In the fall of 2008, in the space of two weeks, his wife cleaned out their bank account and household belongings, leaving him a bowl, a spoon and a mattress, and a note saying, "Call my lawyer," all of this in a house that he owned in the far western suburbs of Philadelphia; two weeks later his mother died. Two days after that he lost his job; a month later his dog of seventeen years died.

I've seen a lot of men, regardless of their circumstances, crawl inside a bottle or under the covers, or go through life zombie-like saying, "Woe is me." Andy took an entirely different tack, which is why he will have my undying admiration. He came out of his circumstances and said, "I'm changing direction." He began to work on a concept his older brother had shared with him. Then he went into partnership in the depth of the recession, in 2009, with one of the designers at PayPal. After three years, in late 2012, they launched an application to rave reviews in Forbes Magazine, related to the $100 billion gift card market.

Their app takes all of your cards: gift cards, credit cards, and puts them on your cell phone (the data is protected and stored in the cloud). If I want to give you a Home Depot gift card, for instance, I can buy that gift card on my phone, bump your phone (if they are compatible), and the value of, say, $100.00, immediately transfers to your phone. You go to Home Depot the next day to buy some fireplace irons and spend $85.00 of the $100.00 (at checkout you call up your credit from the cloud and wave your phone in front of the card reader—there's a bar code on your phone and you're done). You now put your phone in your pocket and forget about the remaining $15.00 worth of value at Home Depot. Two months later you are driving past Home Depot and your phone beeps: "You have $15.00 left on your gift card—come in right now and we'll make that $30.00," because Home Depot knows that if you walk in the door, you're not going to spend $30.00, you're probably going to spend four times that (they have good data that tells them that). And it's all related to escheatment.

Escheatment is a mechanism in law that says unclaimed assets can be claimed by the states, after a designated period of time, whether it's jewelry in lost and found, dormant bank accounts, or unredeemed gift card dollars; the time varies from state to state, and is usually three, sometimes five years. In addition, for Home Depot, or Godiva Chocolates or WalMart, unspent balances on gift cards or any kind of coupon, are considered a liability on their corporate balance sheets. So, in the aggregate, $15.00 unspent represents millions of dollars in liabilities. In the past there was no way of saying. "You have $15.00 in unspent dollars on that gift card you received last Christmas." Now they have that possibility through Andy's app, which is GPS based. Passing any known location, where you have that $15.00 unspent, you are likely to get a prompt, "Come on in and spend it." They can get the $15.00 off their balance sheet by having you come into the store; removing that liability is really the game changer, and for that reason Andy has raised millions of dollars, and hopes to have 10 percent of the market by the end of 2013.

Not long after his dog died, in February of 2009, Andy met a bright, attractive, hard working woman who is in the medical device business. She was living near the art museum in Philadelphia; they were married in September of 2010. They now have two little girls.

Through the 80s I met Judy, we were married, we moved to Texas because the company I was working for: National Resource Management transferred me there. Texas turned out to be life in exile for a couple of East Coasters and their kids. But through that course of time I had the chance to become a battalion commander with the 1st Battalion 23rd Marines in Houston (we were living in Dallas). Midway through that time, I had the opportunity to join a very interesting although nascent investment management firm: American International Management (AIM), run by Ted Bauer, the Chairman from central casting (my description): Boy's Latin, Harvard, Harvard Business School, naval aviator in WWII (he was re-activated during Korea), Cary Grant good looks, clipped Boston Brahmin accent. He knew how to lead and manage, and was honest as the day was long. He appreciated the fact that I was a Marine dedicated to Reserve service, and simply on the fly, when I was activated, he decided to pay the difference between my military salary and my salary at AIM, keeping my family afloat. I started at AIM in January of 1988, as VP of Marketing for the Eastern Region, which was Philadelphia to Davenport, Iowa, Canadian border to Louisville, Kentucky. I was the 89th employee hired.

We made the decision to move back to Malvern, Pennsylvania six or seven months into my new job and nearly fourteen years later, when I retired, a partner of the firm, it was the evening of the 10th of September, 2001. We had gone public; I had benefitted from that: we had gone from $350 million in assets under management to $400 billion with 6000 employees. I had caught the escalator at just the right moment.

I was activated as a lieutenant colonel in August of 1990 right after the invasion of Kuwait (Desert Shield Desert Storm) and reported to Camp Lejeune, North Carolina, and expected to go to Saudi Arabia, but because of my school and college Spanish language study I ended up running a counter-narcotics program based in Honduras, Nicaragua, and Colombia (my major at Rutgers had been History with a concentration in Latin American Studies and Spanish, which has served me well throughout my Marine Corps career). I didn't get to go to the 'Sand Box.' I was away, all told, between Camp Lejeune and Central America a little more than nine months.

I came home on leave the day after Christmas in 1990; it was our custom to take the boys skiing in Quebec (we had booked a month before the invasion). During that trip Judy blew out her knee, which ended up needing surgery. She was covered under Navy Medical: the doctor prescribed a brace which Navy Medical was not going to cover. Ted Bauer heard about that and said, "We're going to write a check for that brace, because I don't want Doug O'Dell's wife to be standing on crutches in line outside a Navy hospital waiting for a brace." That's the kind of person Ted Bauer was; I was able to recount the story publicly (with Ted Bauer in the audience) the evening I retired. He died at 84, not even three years later.

I was singled out for a successful small operation (in South America) whereas I would have been lost in a large successful operation (Desert Storm). Two of the guys, myself and Jim Laster (my number two, came out of that experience years later as General officers (Jim is now a three star General). I returned to AIM, having reverted to Reserve service.

Our boys were starting to go to college; I travelled up and down the eastern seaboard; we moved our sailboat from Sag Harbor down to Maryland and started to put down roots in

Maryland, built a cottage down there which we mostly used on weekends when I was free. Judy was busy in her career as Managing Partner in a CPA firm in Stratford, Pennsylvania (she was a noted authority on Audit and Accounting Theory and Policy nationally). I continued my dual-track career: the investment management business and Operations Officer at Headquarters 25th Marine Regiment in Worcester, Massachusetts. I travelled up there on weekends; shortly thereafter in the spring of 1992 I was selected for Colonel.

In the early winter of 1993 the regimental commander was unexpectedly transferred to a more senior job in Washington; somewhat unusually I was asked to be the regimental commander; it was like working two full time jobs simultaneously. I did that until September of '93, and then went on to become a brigade operations officer at the 2nd Expeditionary Brigade at Camp Lejeune in Jacksonville, North Carolina. They were on the threshold of doing a major NATO Arctic exercise that ultimately culminated in March of 1996 in the north of Norway at the Arctic Circle.

Looking at the big picture (and I am sure this is true in every life), there are complexities of intersections, ironies that are almost impossible to explain. I'll give you two specific examples in my life—maybe this is where the rubber hits the road. First of all, the decision to retire from AIM, after not even fourteen exciting, successful years, where I made a lot of money and enjoyed being part of growing something from nothing, led by a really remarkable guy.

Increasingly, as we got into the latter 90s, and into 2000, the industry I had grown up in, professionally and ethically centered, was becoming commoditized. Professionalism gave way to ego, braggadocio; it was not an industry I was enjoying anymore. My customers were brokers and investment advisors, and they were turning around, making various products: mutual funds of various types: domestic, international, large cap value, growth, that had tremendous track records, making our products part of their clients' overall portfolios. We became victims of our own success: we had more money than we knew what to do with.

We had three tracks: New York Stock Exchange firms, NASD member firms, bank advisor firms; I stayed on the New York Stock Exchange side. My clients were Merrill Lynch, Legg Mason, Morgan Stanley, Smith Barney, Shearson, etc. I found by the late 90s I didn't enjoy my function in the business anymore. I had been promoted to brigadier general in June of 1999, and since the Marine Corps treats its reserve general officers as interchangeable parts with their active duty generals, I found it increasingly difficult to keep my job and my vocation in balance with one another. I made the decision in the fall of 2000, returning from a Marine Corps trip to Argentina right after the USS Cole was bombed, that I was going to retire from AIM; it was time for me to vote for my so-called vocation. I returned to the States, and shortly thereafter in 2001 made my intentions known to management at AIM that I wanted to retire; I was 53. AIM told me they would like me to retire on September 10th.

I decided to devote up to six months a year to the Marine Corps, do some travel and other interesting and engaging things. The Marine Corps had various programs that allowed for short or longer programs for active duty, but the number of officers in any military service is limited by statute; in the Marine Corps, the number of General officers on active duty at any one time is limited to 91, without special permission from the Secretary of Defense. This is convoluted and outdated, as the count is made at the end of the fiscal year. If I'm on active duty from the 2nd of October, 2012 until the 28th of September, 2013, but I'm not on active duty on the 30th of September, 2013 (the end of the fiscal year), I don't count toward the 91 for 2013. I have had situations where the clock has run out on me, and I had to take a 30 day break before I could come back on active duty. During that down period I paid rent for 30 days on my quarters at Camp Lejeune because I was not legally entitled to them. The likes of Dwight Eisenhower or George C. Marshall would be rolling in their graves looking at the complexity which our lawyers and others have devised.

My retirement coincided with the annual partners meeting, a gala that featured 350 partners from around the world. I stood up, made my remarks, told them I would be working on terrorism issues with the Marine Corps (thinking about Latin America, although more recently I was getting drawn into issues related to Islamic fundamentalism). I woke up the next morning and realized my decks had not been that free since I graduated from college 30 years earlier. I had no debts, all our kids were out of college; I had plenty of resources.

The phone rang at 7:47am Central Time in Houston, Texas, an emergency phone call; the second plane had gone into the World Trade Center. They said, "Turn your TV on, and call back when you get oriented." My job before that moment had been Vice Commander of Marine Forces:

Atlantic, Europe and South America, with South America being my piece of the portfolio. Up to that point I was giving the Marine Corps about 90 days a year. Instantly I was on **active duty special work**, ending up in New Orleans that night, where the Marine Corps Reserve Headquarters are located (another officer and I had linked up and driven over); I had a condo there. The next morning I met with Commanding General Dennis McCarthy: Marine Forces Reserve (a 3 star) and another, Jack Davis, Commanding General, 4ᵗʰ Marine Division. I stayed through the end of the week; on Friday, with Jack Davis and a Colonel, we drove East, and I ended up in Maryland that Saturday night, where Judy was waiting. I unpacked and repacked my sea bag.

On Monday of the next week I drove down to Norfolk not having a clue what my future held. On Tuesday morning, September 18ᵗʰ, I was walking down the hall in the Headquarters building, when Lt. General Ayres aide came up and said, "The General wants to see you." So I went in (the General was a blunt New Yorker); he said, "Glad you're here—there's a teleconference tonight I think you want to be on." The subject of the teleconference was the creation of the 4ᵗʰ Marine Expeditionary Brigade (Anti-Terrorism), which was going to take three disparate elements within the Marine Corp: Marine Embassy Guards, Marine Security Forces (security at naval installations and nuclear weapons worldwide), and the Chemical and Biological Incident Response Force (a low key below the radar outfit based in Washington, DC). There was going to be the creation of a 4ᵗʰ element: the Anti-Terrorism Battalion itself.

I went into the teleconference, dead tired, trying not to doze off (it was warm). I was on with Headquarters Marine Corps and the Marine Corps Education Development Center at Quantico, and General Ayres. The meeting broke up around 6:30pm; I went back to my quarters, got something to eat, went to sleep, and was back in the Headquarters building at 6:15am. The aide came down the hall and said, "The General wants to see you." I went in; he was shuffling papers, "What did you think of that conference call?" "Very interesting, Sir." He looked up, "The son of a bitch who has that job is going to have his hands full." He stopped shuffling papers, "You're going to be that son of a bitch."

This was the prime job for a Marine Brigadier General at any point, at any time, at that moment in the Marine Corps, and they were giving it to a Reserve Brigadier General. I attribute that partly to Ray Ayres, also to the guy who was at PP&O (Plans, Policies, and Operations) at the time, and it was not a popular decision. I was right smack in the middle of the bull's eye, so I was sitting in the hot seat, and I was merging three organizations that didn't organically go together. I had to figure out how to synchronize them, and I was creating out of whole cloth assets that were prized by each of the organizations.

In retrospect, I was meant to do that job; by happenstance I made the decision to retire from AIM a year earlier, to clear my decks to be at my nation's beck and call, and that happened the evening before. I woke up the next morning free of any constraint. Because of what I had done the previous ten years, preparing myself in counter-insurgency, I feel certain I was meant to do that job. It was the best job I ever had in the

95

Marine Corps, and I did a good job for three years.

My base was at Camp Lejeune. Judy moved down there; she stayed, off and on for six or seven months; I was gone a lot: three tours in Afghanistan, a tour in Iraq. My stock in trade was rigorous, serious, adult supervised security of high value targets. In Iraq, anything in the Green Zone was a high value target. The Chief of Staff of the Multinational Force Iraq (MFI), a Marine General and friend, asked me to give my assessment: I told him, "This is like Swiss cheese." I left, and two days later the Al Rasheed Hotel was rocketed. A couple people were killed and Paul Wolfowitz, in residence, peed in his pants. That was a Saturday; by the following Tuesday I had an entire FAST Company (Fleet Anti-terrorism Security Team—a specially trained company of 175 Marines) on the perimeter of the Green Zone and had put the Zone on serious lockdown.

I was running reinforcement of embassies with FAST teams that can be deployed in hours to a troubled location (what was supposed to have happened in Benghazi), which I did several times during my watch, almost routinely. I was not the operating authority; I did not make the decision, but I coordinated an operation once the decision was made. In most cases those guys were going in to support the embassy guards (Marines who also belonged to me).

In 2004 I relinquished command to an active duty Marine Corps Brigadier General who had been my deputy in 2001-2. I was selected for promotion to Major General, but because of guys ahead of me not retiring, I languished in limbo for months until I was finally promoted. I left the brigade in

September of 2004 and was assigned to command the 4th Marine Reserve Division based in New Orleans, the largest in the Marine Corps, a little over 21,000 Marines in 106 locations from Maine to Hawaii (the 4th is one of four Divisions in the Marine Corps, three Active and one Reserve). I did not have to live in New Orleans full time due to the numerous locations under my command. Because the quarters were sparse in New Orleans at the Navy base, I would have ended up in the ratty BOQ, even as a General officer, so I bought a condo again; the first time it had been in the French Quarter, and now we bought in the Garden District. This way Judy could come down to a place that was pleasant to be in. In both cases we made a few bucks when we sold; they were turnkey walk-away kinds of places. The second place fortunately sustained no damage from Katrina.

When I took over the 4th MARDIV, it had 2000 troops in Iraq out of 21,000 in the Division. I was on the dot to continue with 2000 to 2500 Marines in Iraq for the foreseeable future. In fact that arrangement became much more systematized in my early days; we knew we were in for the long pull as far as putting fully organized trained and equipped Reserve units as well as Active Duty units on the ground in combat (when I say combat I mean pretty ugly stuff, mano a mano in some cases). It was roughly a month after I took command that we sustained our first casualty, the first of one hundred and eleven killed in action during my watch, and hundreds more wounded. We were in the thick of the fighting in Al Anbar Province.

In January of 2005 I deployed two battalions and associated units to Al Anbar. The office of the Secretary of

Defense had made a decision that no additional force was going to be provided (at least 350 soldiers for security at Al Assad Airbase were needed). The composite force comprised three battalions, of which one was Regimental Combat Team 2 commanded by Colonel Steve Davis, who had worked for me previously at the Anti-Terrorism Brigade. Each battalion gave up a rifle company of 160 for perimeter defense at Al Assad (instead of nominally trained National Guard troops to do the same thing). Normally there were 3 rifle companies plus a weapons company plus a headquarters and service company in a battalion; at a minimum 160 were coming out of a total of 480 Marines in my Regimental Combat Team 2. One of the three understrength battalions, 3rd Battalion, 25th Marines, was in hard combat protecting a 90 kilometer long corridor in absolute Dodge City between Haditha and Hit (this was the corridor for a Sunni insurgency coming in from Syria and elsewhere). By the summer of 2005 I had lost 49 Marines: 22 in 3 days, 15 in one event. I'm not very happy about that.

I went to Iraq in August of 2005 to be with the 325 Marines, to take their pulse, to see how they were doing; they had sustained 49 of their friends killed in action. I wanted to make sure the battalion commander had his head screwed on straight; I wanted to make sure the company commanders felt the same way. When a battalion is down at its heels, that's when they are most vulnerable. I came back from Iraq, passed through New Orleans, wrapped up a few things, thinking I would get ten days of leave after I'd done a couple dozen funerals all over the Eastern U.S., kids killed in action from my units, a grinding experience. I arrived at home on a

Thursday night—on Friday the Headquarters in New Orleans was evacuated in the face of Hurricane Katrina.

Saturday morning my three star boss called, "You need to be prepared to bring some capability back here in case we have an emergency situation." I immediately started looking at units in the periphery of the affected area: Dallas, Birmingham, Norfolk, Tampa, to put together a task force. By Sunday I got the green light to start moving people to areas that were not going to be affected: Jackson, Mississippi specifically. The storm hit on Monday: devastation, surprise events, levees collapsed. Tuesday morning my troops were in Stennis, Mississippi, across the line from Louisiana.

By Thursday I was on my way down there; I spent five grinding weeks doing Katrina. I was Commander, Marine Forces, Katrina. I had responsibility for Search and Rescue, Restoration of Basic Services, especially for the western communities on the coast of Mississippi, from Gulfport to Pass Christian and Waveland, and then St. Bernard Parish, and parts of Plaquemine Parish. We hit the most heavily inundated areas (houses under 14 feet of water, bodies floating everywhere), 2800 Marines involved with all that.

Just when we had our role in Katrina settled out Hurricane Rita came along, so we sortied out to sea to get the troops and the ships out of harm's way: that was another week. We landed behind Rita in Southwest Louisiana, and finally, I came home completely and utterly exhausted.

One week later I was back in the business of commanding the Division.

I retired from Active Service in May, 2007, and retired fully in January, 2008. A few weeks later I got a call from the

White House asking me to become Federal Coordinator for Gulf Coast Rebuilding, which was a three star equivalent job. I was formally appointed in April, 2008.

I did that for the last nine months of the Bush Administration, but there's only one three star job for a Reserve officer, and that's Commander, Marine Forces Reserve, in New Orleans. It was not a job I really wanted; I had been asked if I wanted to put myself in line for the job in May 2002, which meant that I would have had to leave the Brigade—at the time I thought I was doing something important and meaningful—I said no thanks; somebody else got the job. In large measure I don't regret that, although perhaps I could have influenced things in a positive way that didn't happen.

I said earlier the Marine Corps was the third shaping influence in my life; I've never lost faith in the Marine Corps. In retrospect, I wish we had left Iraq to its own devices and finished the business in Afghanistan, because we could have finished Afghanistan for good and for all in 2004 and 2005 rather than having to deal with the vacuum that is going to be left with the self-imposed withdrawal of NATO forces.

The Marine Corps enjoys a place in the minds and hearts of the citizenry as much as it ever has. I think it was General Vandegrift, Marine Corps Commandant (the first four star Marine General, hero of Guadalcanal), testifying before Congress in 1947 who said, "The United States has a Marine Corps, not because its people need a Marine Corps, but because its people want a Marine Corps."

I feel I was meant to command the 4th Marine Division

when I did because, as I said earlier, I set out to make the 4th relevant to the Nation's needs. At the time it was needed, I was the Commander. I don't claim full responsibility—there were many hands in that work—but I was also the son of an amputee who was a former prisoner of war. I was the brother of a man who died young, so I had a unique point of view to deal with the families and communities who were losing young men unexpectedly, and I was in a unique situation to empathize and sympathize with the men who lost limbs and were going through gruesome recoveries at Walter Reed and Bethesda and Brooke Army Medical Center in Texas. I could go to the bedside of a man who was lying there at age 19 or 20, with a limb gone, and maybe an eye out, or with a traumatic brain injury, and with his parents standing beside the bed, relate the experience of my father, with anonymity in the telling of the story, and then I could lean in and say, "That young man was my father, and he lived another 40 years and raised four wonderful children and was the pillar of his community, and I can only wish that for you." I was meant to do that.

I'm a big believer in callings; I wasn't always so, but the older I've gotten, I've come to decide that what you will do in your life will find you, and you better be ready.

Eleanor Sokoloff

Piano teacher for 75 years at The Curtis Institute of Music; age 99

I was born in Cleveland, Ohio; my parents were Eva and Michael Blum. My father was a barber born in Maryland; he had a twenty chair barber shop in Cleveland. I don't think he went any further than elementary school—I never asked him; he was not an educated man. He was dedicated to my mother; she couldn't look at another man. He was at the shop until eight o'clock—we hardly saw him. He did very well. My mother was Eva Eanet, a powerhouse in high heels. Her mother had thirteen children; they had come from Riga, Latvia piecemeal (my mother came when she was fourteen and loved this country with a passion). She spoke Yiddish, Russian, and German, because Latvia belonged to Germany and the next minute belonged to Russia.

In my apartment house in Philadelphia, on the top floor, one penthouse belongs to Milton Rock who gave a million dollars to Temple University and a million dollars to The Curtis Institute; he's a wonderful man—I like him very much. The other penthouse is owned by Mr. Medvek, a Latvian. He was so excited when I moved in—he got on the elevator and gave me his card, "If there's anything I can do for you while you're here, let me know." I never called on him, of course. He brought the Latvian Ambassador to an affair we had at Curtis; he introduced the Ambassador to me, and then he had some kind of entertainment for the man and he invited me; I couldn't go I can't remember why, but I thought that was very nice. He is so dapper—he wears the most beautiful suits.

I was quite young in Cleveland and I had a bone infection behind the ear, multiple ear-aches. In those days they used to blow cigarette smoke in your ear if you had an ear-ache. Behind the ear it would swell and my ears stuck out. I itched and I scratched. Everyone smoked cigarettes and cigarettes were a cure for everything. I had a mastoid operation at nine and the doctor said, "Get her out of this climate." Cleveland had snow on the ground from October until April. My mother used to drag my sister Jean and me to school on a sled (Jean was born twenty-two months after me). It was an icy cold city, dangerous because infections were dangerous; without an operation an infection might go to the brain! There was no Penicillin, and Sulfa didn't come in until our daughter Kathy was a baby many years later. There was no cure—I had Pneumonia three times. My mother read me The Water Babies over and over, such a wonderful story. Besides my sister Jean there was my brother Josh; they're both dead. My brother, nine years younger, died of Lou Gehrig's, and my sister had the weirdest death; she died at eighty. She was always healthy as a kid. I caught Pneumonia because when they took us to Lake Erie to swim I wouldn't take off my clothes, even though I wore a bathing suit. We never took medications. Mustard Plaster was put on your chest and on your back. Now you hardly ever get that kind of Pneumonia where you go through a crisis and you live or you die. Today you get a shot, and it protects you.

My father was permissive; he let my mother do what she wanted to do with me; she loved music. I went to the

Cleveland Institute at eight years old (too late—you don't start the piano at eight). She said, "I think it would be wonderful if you had piano lessons." I said, "Oh I'd like that." All kids say that until they have to practice. Before I was born she had gone to the Cleveland Symphony when she was carrying me because she wanted me to be musical. Don't laugh—it worked. Not only that—it's coincidental the first conductor of The Cleveland Symphony was Nikolai Sokoloff, my future husband Billy's uncle; she was beside herself when Billy walked into my life.

My first piano teacher at The Institute was Ruth Edwards. She died six or seven years ago; I heard from her before she died—that was amazing. I don't know how she remembered, because I was just a kid when she was my teacher. The director of the school was Ernest Bloch. I got my first report card from him. <u>**Very Talented**</u>. My mother was thrilled. Then she fought; she was like a tiger with the public school, "Let her out early—she has to practice." She was so powerful as a mother and as a protector I got out early. So I'd practice, and the music teacher who played horribly would make me play in class, which was a good experience, taking up time so she wouldn't have to do any teaching. I caught on fast; she couldn't play worth a damn. Her piano was dreadful, out of tune, and she played all wrong notes. Her way of teaching music was to play recordings and have you identify what you were listening to, things like Aida. Never taught anyone how to read music which is what they do now.

My father was successful running his barber shop at 105th and Superior, and we had a lovely home. Amazingly, The

Cleveland Institute was in someone's house. I remember my first concert was in the Statler Hotel; I played Ernest Bloch's pieces—he wrote a wonderful collection of children's things called **Enfantine**, and his daughter who was an artist did all the illustrations—fabulous bunch of pieces. Six months study and I was in the recital. But I really started too late to have a concert career—I really did. Today these kids start at three years old and they're marvelous by the time they're ten. In China they start them early, and you talk about Tiger Moms! They make sure those kids practice and the kids are so respectful. There are three people in their lives they worship, their parents and their teacher, any teacher. The teacher tells you to do something, you do it, no question. Our kids don't want to practice. They are so inferior to the Chinese it's sad.

My father gave my mother money for a maid, but my mother took that money and paid for my lessons. My father, I don't think he liked music, even though he went to the concerts. My mother loved music; she had the first recordings that were ever made. You put on the recording and before you could even turn around it was done. It's so amazing how far we've come in a hundred years, because I'm almost there.

Anyway, they asked me to play the next concert—I was such a big hit! I put my hand in an ant hill (I didn't want to play). I figured I've done my duty; I've played six months. I had blisters so bad I couldn't close my hand. My mother was angry but it hurt so she couldn't punish me. I told her why I did it, but she said, "You have to get over that kind of nonsense." She wanted me to be a performer; she wanted me to be a concert pianist. That was her dream. She was living through me vicariously. I didn't know that at the time because

I was eight or nine.

I had another ear operation and the doctor said, "You have to get her out of Cleveland; she'll get it in the other ear." So we went to Florida, the whole family. Florida was booming. My father gave up the business in Cleveland; we never went back. He took that money and invested it in Florida. Everybody was mad for Florida real estate. Even my mother's family gave him money to invest. They wanted to get in on this big boom too, in Boynton, Florida.

We lived in Miami, at that time a desert when it came to culture! There was a Miami Conservatory—my mother thought that would be the place. She went and paid for six months ahead of time and then took me for a lesson. She was furious—it was relaxation exercises. She took me out of there. She found a woman by the name of Mana Luca, very well known in Florida. She had studied with a wonderful piano teacher and was a very rich woman because she had married the owner of a department store. She even had musicals in her home once a month. Mana Luca told my mother she had just the person for this talented child; it turned out to be a friend of hers, a very kind loving woman who didn't know a damn thing about teaching a talented child.

When we lost everything in Florida in 1924 (the boom turned into a bust), it really started with a hurricane. We knew nothing about hurricanes, and the only notice you had was a black flag hoisted over the post office. It turned out to be a terrible one. They had told us to board up our windows. My father said, "What for?" Well, water came in under our door, blowing was horrible (we were up all night), and then all of a sudden the sun came out—everyone went outside. The people on our block said, "This is nothing." We were in the eye of the hurricane, and then it came back again. It was worse than before.

Miami is on the Bay of Biscayne. Big ships had come up on the streets. One of them was on my father's street; business stopped. Then things really got bad. In the afternoon, I was supposed to be practicing when my mother went down the street to my father's shop to collect money to buy food (my sister would be preparing vegetables for dinner—I remember there were scarcely any potatoes to peel). We lived hand to mouth.

My father lost all the money from my mother's family. We moved to Washington where they all lived (my mother's idea) and they sued him! The judge threw it out of court. My teacher, Felicia Rybier, followed us. Of all the cities with business problems, Washington never had any, never ever has had financial problems—you know why? Turnover; there's a constant movement of people who haunt the government, lobbyists. That's why Washington is a complete success. Real estate people have a booming business, constantly selling, turning it over. My father immediately got himself a shop. We went into debt but he did it, even though he had problems with the union (he was scared—they were going to kill him!). He paid better than the union and anyway the barbers didn't want to join. He ended up by doing very well and then he got sick just before I went into high school; I was thirteen or fourteen.

Again, my mother was in the principal's office. She got me out early to practice for my lessons with Felicia Rybier. Then my mother heard about The Curtis Institute of Music—

that became her dream. She told Felicia, "Let's get ready for Curtis; let's prepare to try out." My teacher pushed me for all she was worth. The more she pushed me the more students she had. By the time I was sixteen (it took three years; I really got down to work), I had played a lot of local concerts. I even had a fan group and I was on the radio! So I applied to Curtis, even though my father was against it. He read a scandalous story in the newspaper about Josef Hoffman, the Director, who had two children out of wedlock with a pupil (he finally married her). In those days that was a scandal. As always, my mother had the powers of persuasion. I needed two important signatures, teachers or outstanding musicians on the application. I remember going to Juilliard in New York City, and the head of Juilliard listened to me and signed—he wrote a letter. He knew we couldn't afford Juilliard where you had to pay. Of course my mother came to Philadelphia with me for my audition.

There was a national broadcast every week from The Curtis Institute, and what I heard was amazing. I was terrified, and it turned out in the end I had three auditions! A lot of other people were taking auditions, mostly seventeen and eighteen year olds. I listened—no way I was going to get in. There were a lot of piano teachers at Curtis; piano was a big department especially because the director was a pianist. My first audition was with two of them, and the next was with another three. Then came the finals, with Mrs. Bok, the founder, and Josef Hofmann, the director (he taught also). At one of the auditions they tested my ear (intonation), and I couldn't hear beans. They played an A and I thought it was a

D sharp. I had never had a theory lesson, I never had been tested, and I don't have perfect pitch. I had no idea how to find relative pitch. When they told me I was accepted, you can imagine my mother. I got a letter in the mail. I was accepted because, even with my limitations, I was talented. You know what talent is? 99% effort and 1% talent. It's like you have a pretty face, you're born with it, but with talent, you have to work with it. Now it's different. We have come so far with technique that ten year olds can come in and play Chopin etudes; something has changed. We used to sweat over these etudes. Now they come, these little babies, and they play like I don't know what; amazing to say, but they have so much equipment.

I had not graduated from high school, but when I was back home after the audition, I went to summer school and graduated so I would be through with high school when I went to Curtis, age seventeen. But where was I going to live? My mother was scared to death to let me come alone. But she found the Rebecca Gratz Club for poor girls at 6th and Spruce in Philadelphia, room and board eight dollars a week. We were in the middle of The Depression—1931; men were selling pencils on the street. There were bread lines, people jumping out of windows. Rich people had lost everything. Banks closed—you couldn't get a nickel of your money. One dollar for a steak dinner!

I had two roommates; I was given a little spinet in the corner of the room. I couldn't practice at Curtis, too busy there. In those days they only had that one building; there were practice rooms downstairs, but I was a new student. Boris Goldovsky, a pianist and conductor, Abrasha Robofsky, a singer, they were fellow students, part of a group. They would wait downstairs for the girls; they would try to date the new ones, or they would pinch you or something else. They were awful and I was terrified. Boris used to call me Dimples.

Half of the faculty was having affairs with their students! Later, when I was a teacher, one of the girls came to me and said her teacher was going to throw her out if she didn't sleep with him; she was crying, terribly upset. So I went to Mr. Zimbalist, the Director. He sat me down in a chair, face to face. He was like a father. He said, "My God, what will I do?" I knew what he was saying. That teacher was the only one in the whole United States at that time for that instrument. He was an awful man. Mr. Zimbalist went to the teacher and told him he was a naughty man. He responded by throwing the girl out—isn't that awful? But that was prevalent, that sort of thing.

My teacher, David Saperton, was sleeping with a student from California (I don't remember her name). He was a son-in-law of Leopold Godowsky, a great pianist. Saperton was the teacher of Jorge Bolet, also a wonderful pianist. But Bolet was a homosexual, and at that time, a homosexual was like a devil. Saperton said to me Bolet was "on the fence, and a little push…" I didn't know what he meant; I didn't know about homosexuals. But people were of the opinion it was something that people made you do, one little push. Turns out in the end Bolet died of AIDS.

I was thrilled to be at The Curtis Institute. I had never been away from home, and there were these wonderful handsome Russian men, students. One of them was my first date. But I had no great respect for my teacher. When I took a lesson, David Saperton looked out the window at Rittenhouse Square the whole time, didn't bother to correct me. I learned very little from him. I learned more from Billy Sokoloff, who became my husband, than from anyone else. And after that first year David Saperton threatened to throw me out (at Curtis you are on probation the whole time).

In those days, every year, each teacher was given a whole evening; they would present their whole class. So I was always on the program. Josef Hoffman came to every concert. You were nervous because there were students who had sensational techniques, like Jorge Bolet, techniques I didn't have, but I made music; I felt the music always. Hofmann really liked my playing—he came to me and said so. He wasn't particularly nice; he was brusque with everybody, but he did tell me it was very good. Saperton was Hofmann's old pupil, so I survived. I was at Curtis from 1931 and I graduated in 1937, but in '36 I was put on the faculty. Imagine! My teacher must have been so shocked. Then during the war Mr. Zimbalist, the Director at the time, dismissed a lot of teachers—Saperton was one of them.

I said to my mother after the first few years, "Let me live in a family; I have to get out of that place." There was a Curtis violinist who lived on the top floor at Rebecca Gratz; she had Epilepsy at a time when there was no medicine and she would have a fit and start shrieking. Girls were working in the department stores, making maybe seven or eight dollar a week and paying Gratz close to that; fortunately they received breakfast and dinner. It was a terrible time. My father had contracted TB and was briefly in a sanatorium. He came

111

home, told them he would rest at home, and he went right back to the shop, right back to all that dust, dirt and hair.

My parents finally agreed I could go to someone's home on 17th street, Mrs. Werbell. She had just lost her husband but she was a lab person. A lot of doctors brought lab samples to her. I lived upstairs and there was a singer on the top floor. Mrs. Werbell's sixteen year old son had a gun and he was nuts. He had illusions he was a baron. The police caught him once; he was in the middle of the street shooting. I stayed there maybe two years, but I was frightened. I did have a big wonderful room with sliding doors, a bed and my piano, a good piano not the spinet.

By this time I was already established when I moved from there to Mrs. Trout on Pine Street who had one son and three daughters and had just divorced her husband. She had seen better days, but she fed us and we loved her. She lived on the money we paid her for rent. She bought a secondhand bed and I woke up one morning covered with bites: bedbugs. That was my first experience; I never had them again. She was horrified she had done that to me; she called an exterminator and he did the bed and the whole room. That's when I started to have a lot of boyfriends, before I met my husband. Another girl from Curtis lived there, a composer from California, and she became my friend. It was rumored she was having an affair with Scalero, the great composition teacher. He taught Menotti and Barber and he was an interesting man, but old, very old. She was seventeen or eighteen, lovely and intelligent! She went back to California; I lost touch. So many girls had talent, but there was no place for them. Women still have a terrible time in our field, especially at the top of the field. There is one woman pianist at the top who is really great and a few violinists, that's it!

At Curtis we had loads of violinists because of the orchestra; Stokowski, Mlynarski conducted, big names, always a great orchestra. But we didn't do public performances like we do today. We did radio broadcasts from the school. Now people come because it's a great orchestra. The piano department was smaller. From the first, I had my eye on a piano student by the name of Vladimir Sokoloff; he went by the nickname Billy. He was the handsomest guy you ever saw; how he looked when he was nineteen, twenty—wow! He looked like a movie star. His brother in law was a violinist in The Philadelphia Orchestra, and Billy lived with his sister and brother in law at 10th and Spruce. Their father had come from Russia to Connecticut; Billy was born in New Haven and was brought up in the Bronx (New York City). Nikolai Sokoloff, the conductor, was his uncle. His father was a self-taught painter; to make a living he painted houses. His mother Clara came from Romania; all her life she was a frustrated business person. They met in the US.

Billy's baby brother Seymour was a clarinet player (he was killed in an automobile accident). All three brothers had talent; the third brother Beryl, was a painter and writer (he turned into a correspondent for a Mexican newspaper). During the war, all three brothers were drafted into the Army, to different places. For instance, Beryl was in the Far East, Billy was down South.

I had my eye on this guy from the first and he paid no attention; nothing. I had a boyfriend who was a violinist and I had others before that. You had to have somebody or you couldn't go places. Zimbalist, after his student concert, always took them out, and they could bring somebody. Two of the violinists, at different times, were my boyfriends; I had given up on Billy.

In 1935, at the Christmas party the last day before Christmas vacation, Philip, my boyfriend at the time, was sick; he asked his brother Barney, an accompanist, to take me to the party. So Barney took me with his girlfriend who was my friend (later she was a big hit in the movie business). They were dancing and I'm standing in the hall in a beautiful dress my mother made me. While I'm standing there someone comes up behind me and runs his finger down my back. It's Billy! He had his eye on me; he just never let on. But there it was, and then he walked me home. In the meantime I have this boyfriend. But he said, "Are you going home for Christmas?" I said yes. He said, "I have an engagement with a blind violinist in Washington. Can I come to see you?" I said, "Oh I'd love it." And I'm thinking in my mind, my god, my mother's going to faint; his name is Sokoloff! And sure enough, she was out of her mind with joy. My father had this crazy idea that every man was out to get his daughters (my sister was also attractive).

Billy came and he took me to the movies; I remember he held my hand. That was the beginning.

I had both these guys and I didn't know who to go home with, but I finally got rid of Philip. He wanted to get married and I didn't want to get married; I wasn't ready. Certainly I wouldn't get married to him because I wasn't in love with him.

I married Billy in '36; in '36 I was asked to join the faculty, to teach people piano who played other instruments. That's why I have such an amazing group of people who've studied with me. I have an endless group of people. I'm the only one in the history of the school who came out of that and became a full time member of the piano faculty. And I'm the only woman. There are six men and one woman. Rudolf Serkin put me on the faculty. Why? I brought four kids into The Curtis, four of many I had been teaching on the outside. They were young and they were talented. I used to go to their homes.

My first student on the outside, her name was Charlotte Eskin. She lived in a row house in North Philly—I used to drive there and give her a lesson and drive home. My brother in law Seymour came out with me in a Plymouth convertible, our first new car. I gave Charlotte her lesson; in the meantime it had been snowing, the kind of a snow that in ten minutes you're buried, straight down heavy, a blizzard. We got into the car; I had to go on a street with trolley tracks. I was driving five miles an hour; I'm scared to death. No snow tires, no chains, and right in front of me a big truck stops. I put my foot on the brake and the car slides into the truck, bashed in the whole front, a brand new car that my husband loved!

Billy was standing outside the drug store at 18th and Locust, right across from The Curtis, and I'm coming down Locust Street in a car with a mashed in front (Locust Street was one way the other way in those days); he never said a word. Billy was a saint! I did a few other things through the years. All he was concerned about, was I ok. That's the kind of husband to have. We were married sixty some years when he died.

Billy was playing piano for everybody. He was engaged as Zimbalist's accompanist after Zimbalist's cousin Teddy Saidenberg quit; but he was in Curtis Hall for everybody who gave a recital. He could read any music anytime, and when he was doing that, before he became Zimbalist's accompanist, Teddy's wife thought Teddy was too good to be Zimbalist's accompanist, with all the travelling, so she persuaded him to quit. Zimbalist had Billy accompanying in his class at Curtis so he knew what Billy was like, so he was engaged in '36.

Everything seemed to happen to us when we were married! I had a job for the first time teaching at Curtis. I was overwhelmed. After all, I was still a student; I had another year to go. Billy was finished—he graduated the year before me. He went on tour with Zimbalist right after we got married. We spent the summer before at his house in Connecticut so they could rehearse. Zimbalist's wife, the famous singer Alma Gluck, was a wonderful hostess. She had cancer, and was suffering terribly, but she never showed it when she was with us. That's when I met Efrem Zimbalist Jr., who was kicked out of college. Even then he wanted to be an actor though nobody in his family wanted it. He was with a summer stock company nearby. I thought he was just lovely; to this day he is so very sweet. I said to his mother, "He's so handsome." She said, "Handsome is what handsome does." I never forgot that. She was disgusted with him that summer because he was thrown out of college. His interests were something else. But while Billy was rehearsing, I was down at the pool with Efrem

Jr. We are very close in age. He's still alive. Same beautiful face, with white hair. He had a beautiful wife he loved dearly; she got cancer, a melanoma, and she died in a couple of weeks. He mourned and mourned and mourned. She was only in her twenties.

Billy was touring for six months in 1936, the year we were married. He had met Oscar Shumsky and went on tour with him after Zimbalist. That's why it was so long. When he came back he was formally engaged by The Curtis Institute, to accompany anyone and everyone, as he had done before; he taught as well. Zimbalist played local concerts; the old man was getting older and his career was going down. Then Zimbalist became Director of the school.

I had Kathy, our first daughter, when I was twenty eight, in '42. Billy went into the Army for two and a half years in the last part of '42 and on into '43 and '44. He was in the infantry, in Georgia. If you were from the North, they sent you to the South, and vice versa, to get you away from your family. I visited him; he was doing KP, washing dishes. He didn't go overseas, but his whole unit went. Out of the first group that was sent, they all died.

When your profession is playing the piano, you look for a piano. The only place there was a piano was in the officer's club. When the officers found out that he played the piano they'd have Billy come over. The enlisted men in his unit were envious, mostly Southern squirrel shooters, and they threw him over his foot locker opening up cuts and bruises. But he had made a friend, head of the American Cotton Growers Association. His wife would get Billy to come and play at musicals, and she just happened to be friendly with the sister of General Omar Bradley. When she heard that the unit was going to be sent overseas, she wrote a letter to her brother and he rescued Billy from that unit, sending him to a communications unit, where you had to learn Morse Code. That's where he was when someone realized he should have been in Special Services. You can't imagine how he had hated the seventeen weeks of basic training and the rest. Musicians are not athletic; they don't know anything except their instrument. He lost weight; he went down to a bone, but he was strong because he had to carry a sixty pound pack. He had one leave in all the time he was in the Army. At least he got to see his daughter.

The last six months he was finally in Special Services with Sol Schoenbach, a Curtis trained bassoon player who later taught at Curtis and was in the Philadelphia Orchestra. Sol made friends wherever he was; he was terrific, but he was a very bad boy, this I heard from my husband. We won't go into that. Later Sol told me Billy would get a package from home with a big salami and Sol would come and take it. Before he was discharged, Billy even made a recording of The Cornish Rhapsody. That was Special Services. After the war everyone came home; there were no cars and no place to live. Everything had gone to the war effort. We were in a one room apartment, with our daughter Kathy in the room with us.

We spent every Christmas Eve with friends who had a big place in Rydal, Pennsylvania, a suburb of Philadelphia. This particular Christmas Eve I had just found out I was pregnant with our daughter Laurie, and of course nobody was to know because it was right at the beginning. I sat down in a chair and

118

listened to the drunken idiots performing at the piano, some of them Russian relatives of the owners, the others famous musicians, old friends; it was all noise and fun and laughing. All of a sudden I felt everything coming out and I couldn't move. I'm ruining the chair. But some of the guests were strangers, people only the owners knew. I whispered to one of the wives, a good friend, "Marion, I'm having a hemorrhage. What can I do?" Marion called the hostess. She was one of those people, a great lady who could handle any situation, didn't matter what it was. She was cool, collected, and stood up very quietly. "Will everyone please leave the room." Of course the idiots at the piano thought she was joking, so they stayed there. She hustled me out of the room. The chair was ruined; brand new covering. In the meantime I am having what I think is a miscarriage. The car was brought up; I was taken to the hospital. It was a false alarm. Just a hemorrhage; I had a couple more like it, but only in the first month. Laurie was still there. My doctor said, "Get up if it happens again! Don't go to bed—it's the worst thing. If it's going it will go, if its staying it will stay." She was born in '48.

Rudolf Serkin, head of the Curtis piano department, used to say to Claude Frank and Mieczyslaw Horszowski, both on the piano faculty, "Eleanor is the only piano teacher at Curtis." He said this before I was on the major faculty because my private students, like Susan Starr, had come to Curtis. Don't forget, Susan Starr came in second in the Tchaikovsky Competition! If the head of the school was someone like Gary Graffman, a pianist, he had first choice among entering students. In fact he still takes the best ones even though he has retired as Director.

Many times the pupil asks for the teacher, and often they ask for me. In the old days they gave me the young ones because I specialized in the young. The way I had to work as a kid gave me the insight to teach them. Scales, arpeggios, and music all balanced together. Not Czerny—he is sugar coated. They gave me Czerny but I hated it because it did nothing for me; I wasn't trained well. When I taught Judy Serkin, Serkin's daughter, she called me Mrs. Pischna; that's my exercise book. With the babies, there's an easy one, and then there's an advanced one, progressive exercises. **They change key!** That's my problem with Czerny—stays in one key, which doesn't help you. With Pischna, any exercise you do you have to do in every key. Another one is Joseffy. That's an advanced book that features every possible technical problem. If you finish that book you have a good technique.

In my time, when I was in my twenties, none of the teachers were giving technical exercises, mainly because they took pupils who already had big techniques. When you work with young people you have to work from the bottom up. They didn't know how to teach young kids. They were used to taking students who had wonderful equipment and who played beautifully. When the young ones came who had talent and could hear, they would give them to me.

I was actually a performer because Billy and I played all the time. At first, we started with the two pianos but we didn't want to go on tour. I had my children, and touring, I had seen that with Billy and it wasn't for us. So we went to one piano four hands, played concerts. We were very popular in the area. Billy had a series at The Academy of Fine Arts, a beautiful place. We played there every year and we played at museums and colleges, but we stayed at Curtis and we stayed at home. As a result, I was the only one who was a regular at Curtis. Careers came first; teachers would go off weeks at a time. But that was not for me, or for Billy.

Ten years ago we started seeing a new phenomenon: the Asians, first Koreans, then it changed to Chinese. We had a smattering of Asian students through the years, but nothing like what happened suddenly, later. They are wonderful kids, hardworking, respectful, but they start with Pischna like everyone else, or more likely Joseffy (most are advanced). You give them two or three Joseffy exercises, and next lesson they play them, that's still the difference between me and the other teachers. The others don't listen to that stuff. They want to listen to important works, not exercises. I sometimes give three hour lessons to one student because I hear everything! If they are little, I have one who is ten—she plays scales and arpeggios; she plays Pischna and then advanced Pischna. She has gone through a complete technical program, along with her pieces, her music. It takes about three hours before I hear everything. I have two boys who have gone through the whole program; they play only music for me. But I don't give one hour lessons. What the other teachers do is their own business. And it's different; maybe they come in once every two weeks and I take their pupil on the alternate weeks. I fill in. Officially I have four Curtis students, and each one has a different day, plus my own pupils. I used to teach all day, and a student after supper. I don't do that now; I'm too old. But I love what I do.

Billy's first problem was depression. He went into a very severe depression; I would say he was eighty, maybe eighty-two. For two and a half years he was severely depressed. He kept on working and then one day he came home in tears, "I can't do it anymore." He was in a black hole and I had to watch him all the time (these people are suicidal). When you get a person who is depressed, and for no reason, you can't say what caused it. He took every possible medication; he had a psychiatrist once a week. The psychiatrist would ask him, "How do you feel; is there anything you want to tell me?" "No." "OK, your medication did not work. I'll give you a new medication." Every week a different medication, and even two electric shock treatments (he came out of the depression for ten minutes).

There used to be a place at 39th and Market for mental disorders. They closed it; now these people are out on the street. Billy's problem was called Senior Depression; it comes with age.

Then he had a stroke—he was paralyzed on one side, and he came out of the depression. Go figure! It's something up here (in the brain). I tried to get somebody to help me so I could have him at home. They came to look at the house to see if it was possible and they said no, "Nothing you can do with this house. The doors are too narrow for a wheelchair and you have steps to go up; it's impossible. You find him a place."

First he went into rehab and they could do nothing. They tried and tried, tried to get him to walk, to move—they were wonderful. I was there every day. Finally, I put him in a place, walking distance, a long walk, way over past St. Peter's Cathedral. I used to walk there every day. He was in a double room; he was fed with a tube (he couldn't swallow); it was awful, but he was pleasant, a human being. He came out of his terrible depression, and he's paralyzed—it's ironic. Periodically they would try to get him to swallow food, but every time they tried he aspirated—he would get pneumonia. They never gave up, they tried. He had pneumonia three times; they took him out of there, put him into the hospital. He'd recover and then the tube disintegrated and they had to operate to replace it. A miserable life, and then I don't know why it happened—he died. I was right there. He was eighty-four; I was eighty-three.

When I go, I presume The Curtis Institute will get another woman. Seven men it will be when Richard Goode comes in the fall, and me. This is the twenty first century; women are as important as men and they should be on the piano faculty! It looks very bad, and that's what I told our boss. Whoever it is, I hope they have that ability to teach the less developed talents, the younger kids. Remember what Serkin said, "Who is the teacher here? Eleanor; she is the teacher. She takes them from the beginning, and she creates something." But you know, I don't exactly feel that way. I feel what I'm doing is guiding, because the talent is already there.

I have a new private pupil, a very gifted little boy. But he's been taught so badly. He's American, from Philadelphia; I'm so glad to have him—his name is Carson. He was studying with a bad teacher. When it came time, because his mother thought he was doing bad things, she went to the teacher and said, "I'm afraid we're going to have to leave you." The teacher said, "Whatever you do don't go to Eleanor Sokoloff; she's a bad teacher." His mother told me, "You know, I knew you were the one I had to go to." That teacher had heard my name until she was sick in the face; she didn't want to lose the kid. I've had pupils from her before and I've made something of them, and this boy is easy to change—I'm going to change him. I've already had him since January.

What was he doing wrong? If he has a run, he blurs it all together—it's not clear. He does something instinctive with the music instead of knowing why he does it. First of all, he never played a scale, never played an arpeggio, and when he has these things in the music he flubs them. He got away with it from people who don't know anything about music. He has a wonderful ear; he hears when he does that, but he doesn't care. He's a sensitive boy and it's tough, at his age, to come to me.

He said to his mother, "See if you can find a program on the computer so I can write music." He hears music in his head. And there is a wonderful program on the computer. She got it for him. The staff is there—you can print your own notes; it's really terrific. I found him a good composition teacher, a student at Curtis. He's writing music like there's no tomorrow, so talented. That's good because it gives him a theory background. In the meantime he's made terrific improvement on the piano. I love the mother; she'll do anything for him. He has to pay for one hour, but he gets at least a two hour lesson. I'm very generous with my time. Of course he's nowhere nearly ready for Curtis and I don't make predictions. When he's ready he can try. At Curtis he would get all the musical subjects that he needs, transposition, solfege, all the theory subjects, conducting. You know when it's time. But you don't know what the future holds.

Horszowski played his last concert when he was a hundred—at Carnegie Hall. And then he died shortly after that. He played so beautifully—he was a wonderful little man.

This year is a year of celebration; I completed my seventy fifth year at Curtis.

You never know!

Barney Berlinger

Son of a world champion, athlete, hunter,
engineer, designer, manufacturer

The year is 1862. One of my great grandfathers, Bernard
Ernst, came to America from Germany with six children and
started a smoked fish business in Paterson, New Jersey. Nine
years later in 1871, my other great grandfather was slated to
be part of a firing squad to shoot a French spy in the Franco-
Prussian War. An armistice had been signed between
Germany and France; he went A.W.O.L. to Marseille, caught
a steamer to America and hid under a lifeboat, was fed ham
sandwiches by one of the pursers on board, jumped overboard
at night in New York harbor and swam toward the lights—
that's how he got to this country.

Bernard Ernst prospered, had wagons, and moved from
Patterson to Philadelphia where he died at forty six from
appendicitis. Apparently, he would not allow anyone to
operate except a prominent doctor at Lankenau Hospital. Of
course he waited too long, got peritonitis and died. His
daughter Lucy Ernst, my grandmother, was a Nimrod, an
outdoors girl, good with a rifle—she saved her cousin's life in
the Pocono mountains in a birch grove gathering blueberries;
he was bitten by a rattlesnake on the arm; she took a knife,
sliced his arm, sucked the poison out and was eventually
awarded the Carnegie Medal for Heroism which I have in my
safe today. Lucy married Edward Berlinger (born in 1881),
President of the Kensington Hygeia Ice Company, started at

the turn of the century, a company on the move.

My dad was born in 1908 on Friday the 13th, in March of that year. Grandfather sent my father to Penn Charter (a private school) at 12 South 12th Street in Philadelphia, at the site of the old PSFS Bank building. He had to run to school going through the neighborhoods, to avoid being beaten up; he ran home to Kensington and Allegheny where he lived, a rough tough area. There were times when he did get beaten up, but he ran every day, which is why he later became a great athlete. At Penn Charter he played football, basketball and track and was captain of all three teams; he dominated in track by winning five or six events at the Interacademic Championships: pole vault, shot put, broad jump, hurdles, discus, but he wasn't much in the running events. He was big and strong, not ideal for a runner. His uncle owned Hardwick and McGee, an importer of oriental rugs; they had bamboo poles that went through the center of the rugs. My dad would go down to the warehouse and select his vaulting poles, and that is how he became such a good vaulter. He got the poles, wrapped them with tape, which is what he used from the time he was twelve years old. Just like the book THE OUTLIERS says: if you want to be good at something you have to do it for ten thousand hours. He did just that, vaulted for ten thousand hours. He came close to the world record in 1931 even though he was a heavy man, a big man at six foot two, one hundred and ninety three pounds. That was big in those days, not ideal for a pole vaulter.

Dad graduated from Penn Charter, which had moved to Germantown on the outskirts of Philadelphia, and went on to Mercersburg Academy where he was in the same class as

Jimmy Stewart, a student from Indiana, Pennsylvania. He said later that Jimmy Stewart was a great actor but not a very good high jumper, "He would be doing four feet six and I wanted the bar at six feet." He had camped on his athletic prowess at Penn Charter, didn't study very hard, so his father said, "Before you go to college, you go out to Mercersburg and put another year under your belt." To improve his chances of getting into the University of Pennsylvania, he was what is called a PG today at private prep schools (a post graduate). In 1927, while he was still at Mercersburg, he went out to the Amos Alonzo Stagg National Track Championships and won six events for his school. Amos Alonzo Stagg was a prominent track and football coach at the time, and he wanted my dad to go to the University of Chicago; he also was offered a full ride at USC. In those days travel was slow; there were long train rides. He knew there were acres of diamonds in his own back yard and his father was not really into athletics and wanted him nearby. My grandfather was a hunter but he felt my Dad spent too much time in athletics, even though my Dad was setting records all over the place. So off he went to the Wharton School at The University of Pennsylvania.

His senior thesis at Wharton was on the demise of the ice business with the introduction of the refrigerator. His father said, "If it was good enough to send you through Penn—I'm sticking with it." He said, "Dad, you're making a big mistake, get rid of it." In 1932 my grandfather sold the ice business at its peak—eighteen months later the guy who bought it was out of business, because the refrigerator had taken over the ice business. But he had started a gear business Quaker City Gear

Works with two partners in 1918 at Front and Berks Street in Philadelphia, right under the L (the elevated transportation line). He was immersed in the business community, was president of Philadelphia Rotary which in those days was a big deal.

He was hoping his son would follow in his footsteps. But Dad was having so much fun with his athletics he didn't think much about business at the time. In 1929, 1930, and 1931, he won the National Decathlon Championship, and retired a trophy that had been introduced three years earlier; they never thought anyone would win three years in a row. It's about twenty inches high and is in my rec room displayed with medals, citations for world records, memorabilia such as a movie marquee at 39th and Spruce Streets, "Penn Relay Carnival featuring Barney Berlinger," and on the bottom, "Moira Shearer, in Strangers May Kiss."

In 1928 he was nineteen years of age, made the Olympic team, a mere Freshman at Penn. The Olympics were in Amsterdam. He rooms with a Cherokee Indian name of Tom Churchill, a sprinter. Churchill is a man of the world; my Dad is wet behind the ears at nineteen. He doesn't medal in the Olympics that year because it is raining and he can't hold onto his pole. The last night of the games Tom Churchill wakes my Dad up at two in the morning, says, "Hey Barn, let's go and steal the Olympic Flag out of the stadium." My Dad says, "That sounds like a really good idea. Let's do that." They strike a match, flip a coin to see who is going to shinny up the flag-pole that has no ropes (in their infinite wisdom the committee knew the flag was in jeopardy with ropes). Dad loses the toss; he's the guy who has to go up the flagpole, stuck at the top of the stadium (I went into that stadium when I was in Amsterdam on business to share the aura of the place with my father). Anyway, they steal across the infield, up the stairs; my Dad puts a straight razor in his mouth and shinnies up the pole. He tells the story, "I'm up the pole, the wind is blowing, and the pole is swaying. I'm saying: If this pole ever breaks I'm a dead duck." He cuts the flag loose, drops it to Tom Churchill who is standing at the top of the stands waiting for it; Tom Churchill goes down the stairs, across the infield, Dad starts shinnying down the pole, the Dutch police spot Tom Churchill. They chase him (they aren't going to catch him), he's over the brick wall; he's gone. But my Dad is coming down the stairs; they corner him. He says, "I'm a street fighter—I just pick one out, I cold cock the guy, boom, I'm over the wall, I'm gone." Back in the barracks, I light another match, we flip a coin to see who gets the flag; my Dad wins the toss and gets the flag. I have that flag to this day!

In the summer of 1931, upon graduation, Dad was chosen to be one of twenty athletes to be put on a boat and sent to the Union of South Africa for a goodwill tour, competing against South African athletes. One of the South Africans was a Dutch (Afrikaans) decathlon man, and the country thought he was God. My Dad whipped him in six or eight field events. It was six weeks on the boat to get there; he's over there for six weeks, and he's offered six thousand dollars to be coach of the South African track team, for six months a year at Bloemfontein in the North, six months in the South in Capetown (it was summer at the time; in the winter he would be going South where it was warm). That was a lot of money in those days!

130

He was having a ball! But then he received a telegram from my grandfather, "Cut the lumberei." That's German for playing around. "And get back here; get to work." My Dad said to himself, "Well, I guess I've got to go back." And there he is, back in Philadelphia, and his father has him take a job as a bank teller. He pulls a hamstring, can't run, can't hurdle, can't do anything, and loses the opportunity to be in the '32 Olympics in L.A.

In 1930, Bobby Jones, the great golfer, wins the Sullivan Award, an award for the top US Athlete voted by newspaper writers around the nation. He was presented a trophy and a solid gold medal weighing 454 grams (over a pound). In 1931 my Dad beats out Eleanor Holm the great swimmer, golfer Babe Didrikson; he wins the Sullivan Award. President Roosevelt, from then on (it was the Depression) disallowed any medals struck from gold, and none have been struck to this day.

In 1933 Dad and his father and track coach (with grandfather's flask of Four Roses whiskey) take a train out to the World's Fair in Chicago and Dad sets a new one day world record for the Decathlon, the number of points set in one day. Two months later the event became a two day venue; he still holds the one day world record! I have huge scrapbooks, clippings of all this. I have an 11 x 17 scanner at home. I'm going to scan them all, from 1920; they're getting so delicate. That's for the wintertime, when I can't go outside.

Later in the thirties, 1934 to around 1938, he was the University of Pennsylvania track coach. He had been a Penn roommate of George Munger who was coaching intramural sports. In 1936 George came to my Dad and said, "My name has come up for coach of Penn football. If they offer me the job, should I take it?" George was only around twenty-six at the time. "By all means" was my Dad's response. They offered the job to George Munger, and off he goes to create a football legacy at Penn, a sixteen year history of great winnings. He had sixteen all-Americans; they were a nationally ranked team. In 1952 he wanted to retire; Penn didn't want him to retire; they wanted him for one more year but he saw what happened when Penn tried to get into the Ivy League, no more recruits. Steve Sebo came in 1954, a backfield coach out of Michigan State, and opened with Duke; they still had a very heavy schedule but no material. Penn went twenty-seven games without a win (zero and nine three years in a row).

It is interesting that my father never played football at Penn, since Lawson Robinson, the track coach, had said "You have two choices: you can play football but you are going to get banged up, and you won't be able to train for the Olympics, or you can go all track and field, and qualify possibly for the Olympics." Dad chose the latter. He was World Champion but he never won an Olympic medal.

In 1936 my father married a girl who had graduated in June from the Philadelphia School of Industrial Art, my mother; she married Dad in September. Her father was the secretary treasurer of the hunting club in the Poconos my Grandfather Ernst had started in 1900 by buying three thousand acres of timber land that included two lakes. Frederick, my other grandfather, Mom's father, was president of the club for thirty seven years. The club, now two thousand acres, is still there. I go up there: my sons go up there; they are the fifth generation. But I'm not hard core like my Dad for hunting and fishing. I don't shoot birds anymore. I have a deep appreciation for nature; I want to see it. I don't have any desire to shoot deer, and when I go bird hunting I don't carry shells in my gun.

Mom was a gifted pianist and artist and a kind person who, my father said, would not pull the wings off a fly. She was tolerant of my Dad's wanderlust; he hunted all over the world. Every two years he was off and gone sometimes for ten weeks. He had a good deal of common sense in running a business, the gear company (he became president in 1953); he worked there as general manager through the war years, and the company did well, making tank sighting mechanisms (there was a lot of gearing in the Norden Bomb Sight), accurate, small, servo type gears. There were around a hundred employees, and later in the sixties as many as three hundred. Dad had no formal engineering background, but he had an inventive streak in him, and he had men who could execute his ideas on new devices, new ways of checking things, cutting gearing and such.

I was born in 1938. Memories of my early days were during the war; I used to ride with my Dad to Front and Berks Street on a Saturday when I was five or six. I would sit at a typewriter, print soldiers on the typewriter with his secretary while he was out in the shop making sure all the parts went out on time (during the war they worked Saturdays). When he went on the hunting trips I would miss him; I hated to see him go. He was off to British Columbia, hunting mountain goat, black bear, sheep; he would hunt anything it was legal to hunt.

He could afford expensive trips and had trained the company hierarchy so he might leave for eight or ten weeks. First time I went with him to Africa we were gone ten weeks. Don't forget, in those days it would take four days or more to get there, by plane, by slow plane, not by jet.

I was sent to Penn Charter in 1944 when I was six years old; it was a disciplined education, all boys. A professor of Algebra would pick me up in the morning with three or four others, take me to school from Elkins Park outside Philadelphia (we lived in the suburbs, next to an arboretum, the Curtis Arboretum—it's still there). Gas was at 12.9 cents a gallon; we would pay him five dollars a week; he was our ride. When gas went to 15 cents a gallon that was a big rise! From the beginning my Dad decided I was going to be an athlete; he was dictatorial in a way, but in a subtle sort of way. He was encouraging and I did just about everything he wanted me to do.

The fact that he didn't play football at Penn, Dad wanted me to play football at Penn Charter. In the early years it was a struggle for me; I was big so I always played with guys who were a year or two older than me; in those days they would really lay the wood to me. The seventy pound team started in fifth grade but I was never put on a seventy pound team—I started on an eighty pound team! I was always a pound team ahead of my peers. I never told my Dad how hard it was; I just gutted it out. I was a tackle and then I became an end. When I got to the one thirty fives in ninth grade, I started coming into my own. I got stronger; I trained a lot (Dad showed me how to train). I used to score well in the gymnastics event, so many points for a chin, so many points for a dip on the parallel bars, how high you could climb on the rope, ladders, all that kind of stuff; I was always two or three, never number one, in the school. I had a chin bar at home, on the third floor coming down the stairs; every morning I would practice. When I got to school, especially in the wintertime, I was in the gym training. I was ok in my studies; I got honors many times, not high honors, but honors. I was an only son. My Dad had plans for me; I felt the pressure, always. I had two sisters, Linda who was two years younger, and Gloria, six years younger. Gloria fell and hit her head on a rock crossing a bridge in the Curtis Arboretum when she was thirty; she got water on the brain and died. Linda was an athlete, a fairly good hockey player.

By ninth grade my sports were football, basketball, and track. In track it was shotput, pole vault and high jump; later I set the school record in the pole vault, and I could win most meets in the shotput and the high jump. My Dad tried to make me an Olympic athlete and I had aspirations to become an Olympic athlete in the Decathlon, but I didn't have his speed; when it got down to running the four forty, the hundred and twenty high hurdles, the hundred meter dash, I wasn't fast enough. I wasn't that good in Javelin and Discus. However, in 1957 in Bakersfield, California, I was ninth in the country at the Nationals. Dad was my coach. Because he could size people up as to their athletic ability, he knew going in I didn't have the speed. When I got to college at Penn, I had some good marks in school; he was proud of that.

In 1956, when I started at Penn I played football on the Freshman team. We had three games that year, won two of them and tied Cornell in Ithaca 0 to 0. I was captain of the team that one day—I was a tight end. Most of us played both ways, offense and defense. No two platoon system then. I moved on to play varsity for Steve Sebo the next year. I played end behind a senior co-captain Dave Wexelbaum (I played around 50% of the time). We lost the first six games; we played Yale and beat them. Then we beat Columbia and Cornell. Junior year was a little better; it was a five and four season, and I was all-Ivy.

My senior year I was captain; in August I sent a letter to all the players: "We've got to come out of the chute quick. We've got to knock off Lafayette, Dartmouth and Princeton right off the bat to make sure we have a clear shot at the Ivy League title, so get in shape. When you come to Hershey to practice, be sure you're in shape." Those were the days when Penn had the money and could send us to Hershey to camp, along with the Philadelphia Eagles. We had a great team that went out to beat Lafayette 26 to nothing, Dartmouth 13 to nothing, Princeton 18 to nothing, Brown 36 to nine; came up against Navy, tied them 22 to 22. But then we had a big psychological letdown: Harvard came to Philadelphia, to a muddy Franklin field, our home turf, and beat us 12 to nothing. We recouped, beat Yale 28 to 14, Columbia 24 to 3, and played Cornell where we had to win to take the Ivy crown outright, or if we lost to Cornell, Dartmouth would back into a tie with us.

Cornell comes down to Franklin field loaded for bear. Seventeen minutes left in the game and we are behind 13 to nothing. Jack Hanlon, our great fullback, scores. We take the ball again, go down to the thirty-four yard line; it's fourth and 20 on the Cornell 34; 20 yards to go for a first down! We go for it; our split T. George Kovel throws me a pass in the end zone; I leap up and I catch this pass. We kick the point; it's 14-13. In the next ten minutes we score again, twice! We win the game 28 to 13. That was our highlight of the year. And of course my Dad was there. His picture was in the paper, his fist in the air.

In track, during the spring, I set a university record for the pole vault, 14'-4", with a steel pole, not the springy fiberglass pole they use today. It's a different event today, more acrobatic, more like a gymnastic event. In my day it was a strength event, speed and strength. I also won the Heptagonal Championship. On the National level the best guys were doing 15'6". It wasn't until the mid 60s that 16 feet was achieved. But that was with the new fiberglass pole. Recently a Russian did around 19'8".

I finished at Penn and immediately went on six month active duty in the Marine Corp, to be followed by five and a half years in the reserves. I wanted to serve my country, and it turned out my first girlfriend had a father who was a Colonel in the Marines. I enlisted, went to Parris Island, wound up outside of Philadelphia in the Air Wing at Willow Grove after training in Jacksonville in aircraft maintenance; the total commitment extended to 1966, with two week summer maneuvers in Beaufort or Cherry Point, North Carolina, and one weekend a month at the Willow Grove airbase (we had a squadron of jets to service).

After those six months of active duty I started working for my Dad, at first in the shop. The company was in Bethayres, a suburb of Philadelphia, not far from the airbase (they had moved from center city Philadelphia in 1952 during the Korean War, needing room for expansion). My Dad, who loved to hunt, bought a 120 acre hunting preserve in Bucks County in 1961 and moved there from Elkins Park. I was still living at home so I moved with my parents. It was a 40 minute drive to the plant, and I travelled to work with my Dad. We worked together quite well. We had our differences, but you rarely argue with success. We made electro-mechanical mechanisms, essentially gears: anti-submarine warfare devices for the Navy, plotting boards that would plot the path of a submarine from an airplane or from a ship, tank sighting mechanisms for the Army (you want to shoot a gun 4000 yards? Those dials better be accurate!). Sales were $5-6 million.

I had majored in Mechanical Engineering at Penn, so I was one of several design engineers, actually able to design a fairly sophisticated gear. I had good practical teaching at work, but I had the formal background as well and I was fairly good at Math, always looking out for new technology, gearing specifically. I went to Germany in 1975 and licensed a new gear design that we used at Quaker City Gear, a German patent I am still using today to good economic success (the patent by now has run out, so no royalties are paid anymore). It is interesting that other companies can now use the design but they choose not to, due to subtleties in the design and the way it has to be manufactured. They don't care to unravel what we know how to do. We've paid the price, learning how to do it.

Of course there were the hunting trips I mentioned earlier; I first went with my dad in 1952 when I was a 14 year old, to Alaska. I shot a brown bear, a moose, and a mountain goat. I recollect we ate the bear, and we ate some of the moose meat, which is a delicacy. The guide flew most of it back to his home in one of the float planes. His wife made a pie, put the pie in the plane, and that became our dessert. 1954 was Africa, hunting the big five in Kenya and Tanganyika (now Tanzania). The big five consisted of the lion, the leopard, the buffalo, the elephant, and the rhino. We killed a lot of things you can't kill today. I have their skins and heads in my basement. I have leopard and cheetah skins. That trip was 8 weeks. We had the big white hunter, 15 native boys, two trucks, a panel truck, and a power wagon that got us around for hunting. An elephant license was 700 dollars, just to shoot one. In those days you could take the tusks home; they put the clamps on that 25 years ago. Today it costs $25,000 to shoot an elephant.

We went to India in 1956 to hunt tiger and all sorts of Indian game, like the panther, an Indian leopard, a four horned antelope called a chowsingha. That first trip we did not get a tiger. We got 7 panthers, and a bear; my Dad went back in 1968 and got his tiger. I have the head, mounted, and I have the skin. I couldn't shoot an animal like that today. It was very exciting in those days. 1959 was Africa again. 1964 was Wyoming and Utah for mountain lion and bear. That's when I stopped. Now I had 3 kids. Dad continued.

I was married to Valerie in September of 1961. We lived in the carriage house on the farm my Dad had bought 3 months earlier. We lived there 3 years and then moved closer to the company; the town was Meadowbrook. It is where our three sons really started out.

Meanwhile the business was flying high, up to 300 employees at one time. Unfortunately there was a recession in 1984 and we struggled in 1985 and early 1986. In 1986 my Dad and his two cousins (who owned 95% of the business), decided they wanted to sell. We turned things around and the business started making money again selling a lot of open gearing for industrial use, defense contracts (small sighting mechanisms, spare parts and the like). Dad was still running the show and was the major shareholder; I didn't own anything. A former executive of ITT bought the business. I took paper, a 3 year consulting contract. Since I had ideas about what I wanted to do, and I knew where my father was coming from, there were no hard feelings. The buyers thought we didn't know how to run a business; if you want to sell a business, that's who you want to sell to. Dad got top dollar. In 18 months they put it in Chapter 7 bankruptcy; meanwhile I had started my own business.

I went to the bank and got a loan of $100,000. For collateral they took our farm in Bucks County (we had moved there from Meadowbrook in 1978). I was also using the money from my consulting contract to finance the business and then, just like that, they went bankrupt; it all stopped. I was between a rock and a hard place. If I wasn't successful with the new business, the farm, my cars, everything went to the bank.

I based the business on the demographics of the country at that time, where the bubble of older people going into retirement needed ways to get around. The scooter business was growing rapidly, 3 and 4 wheel 5 mile an hour scooters for the walking impaired—we made the trans-axle drives, the differential, that powered them; we had a track record in that product at the old business. I had my own design ideas. In the late 80s the market was taking off. I picked up an existing customer from Quaker Gear; Quaker actually sold me some of the tools before they went belly up. I didn't like the design at the time, but as I now had the customer in southern New Jersey, Electric Mobility, I managed to find another customer that made wheelchairs in Elyria, Ohio, and we started making gear drive systems for them that drove the belt which in turn drove the chair wheels (they had the motor itself).

The first 400 units shipped to Ohio, to Invacare Corporation, were rejected. Everything came back; too much noise. As I had no working capital, we were in deep trouble. You know what happened? My wife Valerie came in and we spent a week tearing those things apart (she got grease up to her elbows tearing gear boxes apart). I scrambled around, had them degreased, figured out what the problem was, tooled, reassembled, worked nights, and got them all back to the customer and got paid. Those 400 systems turned into 36,000 (1000 per month for three years). We were doing $3 million; that got us over the hump. And what also got us over the hump? I ditched the old trans-axle design for Electric Mobility, went out and designed my own scooter differential, based on what knowledge I had, and sold the first run to a scooter company in Central Michigan; they subsequently gave me my first really big order. Now we were rolling; I was on the way. I probably had only 10 or 12 employees. Today we have 35 employees, but we're much more productive. In those early days I would buy a used gear cutting machine, rip it apart, fix it, do it all myself, get the book and cut the gears for the orders. I couldn't afford new machinery.

In 1999 my company ASI Technologies was the biggest producer of trans-axles for scooters in the world (one year we produced 60,000). It was a standard trans-axle that had custom gear ratios and axle lengths. The axle lengths could flex a little bit, and they could have different configurations, and the gear ratio could be different. However, no patents covered our product.

Knock on the door—China comes in: "Mr. Berlinger, we're going to take all your market away in two years; we want you to license that product to us or we're just going to take it all from you." You know what I said? I said OK. They came in; they paid a royalty for two years on the trans-axle design, 20,000 units, and after two years we had 80% of our market taken from us. I was sweating bullets. I didn't know what to do; it was 2002. We had been doing $4 million and the trans-axle was the majority of our product line. We had to re-deploy our assets into products that would not compete with China; that was hard because we were geared up for higher volumes, everything that China wanted: higher volumes, simplicity, make them like cookies.

I had a group I had created, a bunch of guys called The Tech Group, 14 CEO's, all different, no cross-fertilization. I picked two or three of the guys I thought highly of, and I sat down with them. I said, "I don't know what I can do; I have to deep six this company." They said, "Are you sure you want to do that?" I said, "The Chinese are selling their product at 40% less—I just don't know what I'm going to do." So I was going to go bankrupt. I had another guy I had a lot of faith in. He said, "You know your business—you stick with it and pull yourselves up by the bootstraps. Go into other markets, do other things." So I did.

We changed our focus to smaller runs of much more custom types of arrangements. You couldn't go to China and get the custom engineering that some people needed. We got into the floor care industry. You know those big machines that polish floors? We started making trans-axles for The Tennant Company. We took business away from some of our competitors because we had a better product. They came to us and said, "We have a problem; can you solve it? Trans-axles are breaking; we're going to have to recall machines, bring them back to Minneapolis." I said, "We'll re-engineer them for you; we'll make a drop-in. Keep the units out there; we'll ship to you, and the machines will work fine." They asked, "Can you deliver in six weeks?" "Yeah…" I don't know how we're going to do that, I said to myself. And there were thousands. So we started with 120 of their busted up units and we saw the bearings were wrong, the shafts were too little. We knew how to reverse engineer stuff, so that's what we did, to make them better. We shipped the first 120—today they're our biggest customer, 6000 a month all told, and about 3500 of those are for Tennant, different sizes. We ship to Minute Man, other floor care people. We have two UK customers who buy custom designed gear boxes for stair climbing products (where you put a rail up the stairs and ride up). When you get into custom design, China has a harder time, with a 12,000 mile pipeline plus a language barrier. And when you carry a person up the stairs, you are scared to risk problems.

I had two sons in the business from 1998 to 2002 (my third son is a helicopter pilot). One was my CFO and the other was in sales, an aggressive salesman. In 2002, when the Chinese came in, they said, "Dad, all risk, no reward. We're out of here." Now, of course, they wish they were back in the business. I wouldn't take them back. The problem is simple; they already have good jobs; they are not totally satisfied with their jobs. However, in the interim between 2002 and 2012, I developed a disciplined, skilled team, and I don't want to disturb it. I have a board of advisors, two of whom are very good, both retired; one ran a $300 million corporation, the other runs a top-flight accountancy a few miles from here. The two of them, and the President who I have running the company, would run the company for my wife Valerie if I died. I'm the CEO, into long-term planning, machinery. The President runs this place day to day, better at it than I am. He's an engineer from Drexel, been with me for 12 years, paid his dues; the guy is great. But no ownership; that I would not do; that complicates things. I compensate him pretty well and he's worth it. But remember: in manufacturing, we travel economy class. I have nine paid holidays; I come to work every day. I have no yachts. And we always have China behind us. And then we have enough of an intelligence quotient, the company could develop products without me.

To have our feelers and radar out, looking for new stuff all the time, that's what I do. For instance, we've hit on a new area of interest: robots. We are dealing with a company in

New England that has these little robots with two gear boxes—a 44-page specification. We love it because it's highly specked, very electromechanically rated. We created drawings for the gear boxes. The robot is theirs; we supply the drives. They had generation one, but they want a major improvement in generation two. They sell a point of order system for large warehouses: CVS, Best Buy, Kmart, Amazon, huge million square foot warehouses. In the past you had a pick list. The guy goes out, picks this book, picks that book. No more. They put 60 robots in a million square feet—these little robots, and all you have are seven foot shelves, with items on them. You call up for a pair of shoes on your computer or your iphone: I want shoe number so and so. It goes into the computer, the robot gets the job of picking it, goes out to find the shelf, brings the shelf over to the picker, and the picker hits it with a wand for the bar code: Yes, that's the right pair of shoes. The picker hasn't moved; the shoes have come to him. He takes the shoes.

I went into their demo room; they had 40 robots. They look like spiders, buzzing around. You know what? They can't crash into one another. They have to pick up the right shelf, which means that those wheels have to know exactly where they are, all the time, because it's all wireless. And you, Mr. Robot, are in a queue behind these other shelves. Valentine's Day comes; all the stuff that was in the back of the warehouse has to be brought out front, because that's going to be active on February 14th.

These people are software people. They make the robots, but we make the gear boxes. If we make a gear box that draws less watts than a competitor, they don't need as many robots because they don't run out of juice. The robots know when they run out of battery power; they go to the wall and plug themselves in. But the charging stations are expensive, so the more efficient the robot is, fewer charging stations. Our customer has that down to the penny. We know how many watts we can spend to get out of the electric duty cycle; that's our stuff.

The robots have a five hundred pound lifting capacity; we have already started on a thousand pound lifting capacity! They all have a pre-determined acceleration and stop cycle so the shelf doesn't upset. That's in the spec. We have a six thousand pounder on the board for a company 25 minutes up the road from here, JBT (the old FMC). They have their own robot but we're making the gear boxes. We have prototypes up there. This stuff is highly engineered. They had a good gear box to start, from the Japanese, but ours was better or we wouldn't have gotten the job. We are saving them money and giving them a better product.

See what's on the board? That particular gear, the one we lost, may come back from China. We can see our way clear to bring it back because we now have the technology here to do it cheaper than the way they are doing it. Caterpillar is bringing a lot of stuff back from China. And weight is a factor—that old gear on the board costs $2.50 to ship from China, which goes into the cost of the piece.

A democracy is awfully hard to beat compared to a centrally planned economy. Retirement? I enjoy working; I have another little company that works in the wind turbine industry, among others, with new gear technology, a very slow, difficult, complicated effort. I'm faced with a staid (perhaps rightly so), cautious, risk averse industry, because if gears break, bad things happen, very expensive things: the lights go out, liability. That's bad. It's a tremendous challenge of creativity and persistence. I've been in that fight almost 11 years now, and I still don't have my first licensee. I am convinced that my technology is viable, economically sound, and will advance the state of the art immeasurably. Solar costs 24 cents a kilowatt hour, wind costs 7.5 cents, fuel costs 5.5 cents, nuclear costs 3.5 cents a kilowatt hour. Nuclear is the answer. But they don't want to do it because it's going to blow up; it won't blow up. If half the people in the US were engineers, you'd have a lot of nuclear power plants. People get these ideas around the world, from Japan, for instance, and understandably so; on a fault line you've got a big disaster on your hands.

So I've backed away somewhat from wind, and I'm now into Aerospace: air travel, where, saving a kilogram of weight means a lot. It's a ten year program and I'm 73 years old. I formed another company for 1/ liability reasons (I don't want this company dragged down), and 2/ it's a different business. It's a licensing and technology business, not a manufacturing business. Boeing will license from us, then subcontract to one of their good suppliers. We supply the technology; it's an engineering company. We have patents around the world. I have a partner from Canada, a Brit by birth, who divides his time between Canada and Tucson. He is the best Kinematics engineer I know of. Kinematics is the study of motion, and gearing is the study of motion: how they rotate, the stresses, velocity. He is a shareholder, and he is also over 70, a great guy. We've known each other for 25 years. We'll license Boeing or some other company.

Andrea Jenson

A woman for all seasons

My maiden name is Allain. I'm a combination of French and English. My father's family was from French Canada and settled in Lewiston, Maine. I knew only my grandmother from that side of the family; she loved me dearly. My grandfather was much older than my grandmother and died before I was born.

Robert Wilfred Laurier Allain was my father's full name. He was named after the seventh Prime Minister of Canada, and the very first PM who spoke both French and English fluently. He was a moderate who balanced the interests of French and English Canada. My grandmother spoke French and struggled with the English language.

My mother's family had roots in England, and had names like Chase and Littlefield. I didn't know the Chase grandparents very well since they too died when I was quite young. I have vague memories—they lived in Auburn, Maine.

Born in 1915, my father was Catholic. Born in 1916, my mother was Protestant. For some family members it wasn't a happy union when my parents found each other and married. I am very proud of the fact that both of my parents respected each other's religious affiliation and went to church regularly, though separately. Religion was never discussed in our home, but the love that my parents' shared and their tolerance for each other's beliefs, taught me a life long lesson.

My mother died when I was just twenty-nine, my father

seven years later. Sadly, I had very little time with my parents. As my brothers and I have agreed, we didn't have quantity, but we did have quality.

I grew up in Eliot, Maine, on the Maine-New Hampshire border, which is determined at that point by the Piscataqua River. Bridges link Portsmouth, New Hampshire with Kittery, Maine, and Eliot can be seen to the right (going south by car), and extends a few miles north—we eventually lived along the shore upriver. My parents moved to Eliot from Lewiston and Auburn during the war where my father found work on submarines at the Portsmouth Naval Shipyard; he was a metalworker, and he actually engineered a method to safely heat water aboard a submarine. He was recognized for this accomplishment and his photo was on the front page of the Portsmouth Herald.

Though my father held no degrees, he was a consummate engineer. He helped fabricate and then installed the metal steeple at Colby College when he worked for Hahnel Brothers in Lewiston; both the steeple and the company still exist today. Someone recently told me Hahnel Brothers was (and is) the best in their field; that's where he trained. My father spent his later work years at Pease Air Force Base where he was a civil engineer in charge of metalwork and repairs on the base.

Neither of my parents had access at that time to a typical college setting, though both were highly intelligent. My mother graduated from high school with honors at the age of 15, and took a year of post-graduate study. She eventually went to Business School later in life and once again graduated with honors.

My father rarely sat still. He worked all day and then came home and built the houses we lived in—the last house was a comfortable ranch located on the banks of the Piscataqua River. My dad did everything on that house except the plastering. He framed, shingled, built the cabinets, the granite fireplace, did the plumbing and electrical. I was twelve when we moved into the garage, where we lived for three years while he was finishing the house. My two brothers were in college at the time, seven and nine years older; they came home summers and some weekends to help my dad. They learned a lot of skills from him, as did I. I too have some of my father's tools and still use them. I have a certain amount of talent in working with wood, and I sometimes feel as though my dad's hand is guiding mine. I enjoy his legacy of straight and level and his spatial ability.

My parents were in many ways, opposites. My father was the civil engineer; my mother a scholar who had 5 years of Latin. I recall my father telling me about how he had taken a class in drafting, and my mother, who my father respected greatly for her intelligence, was very helpful to him in the beginning. But to my father's enjoyment he told me, "I left her in the dust," My dad had found his element.

A woman who loved to read, my mother launched us all in that direction. Recently I funded the placement of a tile on the walkway into the William Fogg Memorial Library in Eliot, celebrating my mother's devotion to learning, and the many times that she took my brothers and me there. It reads, "Evelyn Chase Allain trod this path."

My parents had a great marriage; they truly loved each other and all of us. We were a close family and we did things together. My brothers and I played basketball at Eliot High School, and our parents very rarely missed a game.

We had boats: lobster boats, power boats, a sailboat, and then THE MEN decided to build a speed boat. My two brothers, Stan and Lee loved speed, my father too (my mother and I, not so much). They built this ten foot long Class B Racer in the garage, a tiny boat painted bright red. They found plans in a magazine, probably "Popular Mechanics." A Super 10 HP Wizard engine made her fly.

It was a tiny craft and was designed to hold only two people. One pointing it.... the other holding on for dear life! The story goes that my mother rode in the boat only once, and to this day my brother Stan claims that her thumbprints were embedded in the paint.

And then came the accident. Older brother Lee was painting houses down on Kittery Point during the summer, and Stan decided to pick him up in the little boat after work; he had a girl with him. They went down the fast-paced tidal river, picked Lee up at the dock and headed back out into the harbor. As they turned up river toward home, they were hit with a wave. The boat flew up in the air and capsized. My brother Lee was on the bow and when he saw the wave coming, he jumped off hoping to avoid a mishap. Stan eventually surfaced safely, but the girl was not immediately in sight. However, she then bobbed to the surface, to their collective relief. In a short time, the Coast Guard picked up the soaked and chilled crew and towed the little boat in. My parents got a phone call saying their kids were down at the Coast Guard Station, and would they please come and pick them up. Relieved, but to my parents' displeasure, the story made the AP and the nightly news. My father, concerned that his sons might be fearful of the water as a result of the accident, rapidly flushed the engine with freshwater. He had it operational within hours, and my brothers were cruising the Piscataqua the next day, perhaps a bit more carefully....

Athletics were important to all of us. And like my brothers, I also played basketball. In fact I saw my basketball coach recently. Robert Perham is now eighty-six and he was a key person during my high school years. We had a basketball hoop in the driveway, and my dad, my brothers and I would go out and shoot after dinner, playing HORSE and Around the World for hours.

I was almost a tomboy—we lived in the woods and on the water. I am reminded on occasion that I asked for a pair of stockings and a hatchet for my 13th birthday.

Back then and still today, I have a Best Friend. Danny Taylor, now known today as Danelle Taylor Hughes, and I explored our world together beginning when we were twelve years old. We roamed around the area, climbed trees, stole Lilacs for our mothers, pondered life, and spent many hours aiming a basketball at a hoop. Those years we shared together were just short of idyllic.

Once Danny and I were in high school, we both played basketball. Though we were on the varsity team as high school freshmen and sophomores, we hardly ever played. At the end of our sophomore year, the team comprised of juniors and seniors had won 104 games in a row. A very tough act to follow.

AN IMPOSSIBLE ACT TO FOLLOW

Coach Perham reminded us at a recent mini reunion that the team that followed abruptly ended the 104 game-winning streak. Danny, Elissa Brown Thibodeau, (our center), and I were now playing "first string" on that team. We promptly lost what would have been game #105. Mr. Perham recalled that at the end of the game, we came back to the bench crying. He told us that it upset him to see us so unhappy, but he reminded us: "You learned from it." We lost one more game that season and then we never lost again. Mr. Perham brought life to girl's basketball when there was so little emphasis on girl's sports.

During the long winning streak, the Eliot High School girls' basketball team beat all of the teams in our area in Southern Maine, and was invited to play a game against Ayer, Massachusetts in the Boston Garden prior to a Celtics game. I was a freshman at the time and after we were way ahead on the scoreboard, I was sent in at the very end of the game. Promptly, I was fouled and headed to the foul line. I scored one point in Boston Garden! What I learned from Mr. Perham, a quintessential coach, was how to win, and how to lose gracefully. As he would say: "Because you're not going to win them all."

I was always an honor student, as were my brothers. My older brother Lee, became an Engineering Physicist (or as some would say, a REAL Rocket Scientist); he completed his master's degree in Electrical Engineering at Villanova. My brother Stan and I are very much alike. Lee is the more pragmatic of the three. Stan and I always say that unlike us, Lee has everything figured out.

After a successful career working with major Fortune 500 companies, Lee is now active in the local area of Virginia where he lives, studying the farming of oysters in Chesapeake Bay. And not long ago he was pictured in the newspaper teaching teens how to build solar panels. He has always shared his knowledge with others, especially young people.

Stan is tall and outgoing; he was a good basketball player and at 6'3", he got a lot of exposure in the local papers. He worked for many years in the insurance industry in Boston, and eventually moved on to a Reinsurance firm, Balis and Company, in Philadelphia (owned by C. Wanton Balis, Jr, a prominent Philadelphian). Mr. Balis hired my brother and really appreciated his well-spoken New England ways and his great sense of humor. Mr. Balis all but adopted Stan, and after several years my brother became chairman and CEO of Balis and Company. He travelled all over the world, working with major insurance companies, including underwriters at Lloyds of London.

In addition to being Chairman and CEO of Balis, Stan was on the board of Guy Carpenter, a pre-eminent Reinsurance brokerage firm, and Vice-chairman until the year 2000, when he retired. Besides an office in Philadelphia, my brother had an office in New York City in one of the twin towers of The World Trade Center. He retired the year before 9/11.

As a student at the University of Maine, Stan had been in ROTC and was the president of the military honor society: Scabbard and Blade. He graduated from college, came home, and almost immediately received his orders from the U.S Army. He was sent to Germany in the early sixties when the Berlin Wall was still a hot issue. My mother made the decision that we were going to visit him; she said: "I'm not going to go two years without seeing my son." I was a junior in high school and got permission to be absent from school for three weeks and travel to Europe. Danny's parents agreed, and she got the same permission slip.

On a crisp fall day, my mother and father, and my friend Danny and I boarded an airplane headed for Munich, Germany. Stan met us at the airport and we began our adventure. We saw Heidelberg and Munich and then Stan drove us to Paris. Mother had done a lot of studying about where we should visit. This would be our grand tour of the Continent. We rarely stopped to breathe. After a week in France, we drove back to Germany and caught a train to Rome where we had an audience with the Pope, along with thousands of others in St. Peter's Square. After touring the City, we re-boarded a train and began the journey north and made our way to Switzerland, and laid our eyes on the Matterhorn. From there we returned to Germany and finally back home. It was an adventure that Danny and I will never forget.

Mildred Obrey lived to be a hundred and one. She was my English teacher at Eliot High School, and encouraged me to enter a nationwide speech contest called: The Voice of Democracy. I was to write a speech of a certain length explaining what democracy meant to me. My dear mother and Mrs. Obrey had to listen to me recite it over and over again. I submitted my entry to the Voice of Democracy Contest and my speech won first place for the State of Maine. I won a trip to Washington, DC, and got to meet several dignitaries, including the incumbent Secretary of State, Dean Rusk. However, I didn't win the National award. But because I had won the contest for the State of Maine, my speech was printed in the Congressional Record. I was very proud of that accomplishment. However, someone once said to me: "They will print anything." But never the less, those were my words that were printed.

My family wasn't poor; we were comfortable. (Though my older brother Stan would lead you to believe that he grew up in poverty while I grew up in wealth!) My brothers and I all went to college. And everyone worked; we all had jobs in the summertime. One of the first things the boys had to learn was how to haul lobster traps. Our father purchased a lobster boat and made certain that my brothers had that experience. Over the summers, Stan worked at a local mill called Fibertex, and Lee was delivering milk at four AM. I didn't haul lobster traps, but in high school I worked Friday nights and Saturdays at J.J. Newberry. Like my brothers, I had to save money for college. My parents bought Savings Bonds; they had stacks of Savings Bonds squirreled away for our education. The deal was that they would pay for half.

We all went to the University of Maine for our undergraduate degrees. My class in high school was very small and fit me too snugly. What I needed was a larger group of people, and the college campus at Orono felt just right. Quickly, I became involved in a lot of activities. I ran for office, was bonded and served as Treasurer of my class for two years. By my junior and senior years I became a more serious student and became a Junior Resident, managing a floor in the dorm, along with my dear roommate, Evelyn

Eachus Sargent. She was on one end of the floor and I was on the other. We helped the incoming students settle in and pretty much provided guidance to the others on the floor. I joined a sorority and was active in Pan-Hellenic and philanthropic activities. At the end of my sophomore year I was tapped for an honor society at the University of Maine; I became a Sophomore Eagle (they wake you up early one morning and tell you that you have been selected). The Sophomore Eagles serve the University by welcoming and assisting the incoming freshman.

My college roommate and dear friend today, Evelyn Eachus Sargent, had been valedictorian of her class in high school. She is very, very bright, and was a Pre-med Major. She was the serious one who studied. I was a little less so. Evie's studies took her to Bar Harbor where she has had an excellent career in research at Jackson Laboratory. Evie and I bonded over those four years together. You might say we coalesced—she turned me into a better student and I sometimes brought her out of her books.

You were required to declare a major in your junior year in college. I chose to major in English, though sometimes people asked me what I was planning to do with it. To their amazement, I told them that I had no plans to teach. However, over these many years, I have often laughed at that question. As I made my way up through my business career, I discovered that my degree in English, gave me the ability to express my thoughts clearly and concisely. The communication skills I developed at the University of Maine have served me well.

During each summer while in college, Danny and I waitressed at a standing room only steak house in Kittery, Maine. I learned how to balance a tray. That taught me how to work, which assured me that I would never starve to death. My friend Danny and I zipped along to work day after day in her parent's open-door Jeep. Working together made it bearable.

That job gave me nightmares every summer. Once we began again, Danny and I found ways to enjoy the time there. In those days, we wore bobby-pinned caps and little green aprons over a plain white dress. I would be taking an order and Danny would come by, tug the apron strings in the back, and the apron would begin falling down to the floor, leaving me scrambling to pull it up. No way around it though, it was a strenuous job. You had lobster all over you most of the time. But Danny and I made the money we needed.

At the end of my junior year, I was chosen to be an All Maine Woman, an honor society at the University of Maine based on a woman's scholastic record and her involvement in university life. That recognition was the pinnacle for me at UMaine.

After finishing college I felt as though I needed to spread my wings, and that trip to Europe while in high school gave me ideas. I decided to return to Europe before searching for a job. My parents kindly loaned me a thousand dollars and Pam Solomon Reid, another friend from college.... and I headed off to Europe for three months, Eurail Passes in hand. When summer came to an end, reality finally reared its head, and I returned to Eliot and began to look for work. That European trip gave me the confidence I needed for my launch into the business world. I learned that I could find my way around.

My job search led me to Massachusetts where I found a position at a hospital in Webster, twenty miles south of Worcester. A very dear man named Bernard Gagnon, the Administrator at Webster Hospital, was searching for someone who knew something about writing and could learn about personnel management. Completely untested, he gave me a chance at this new position, and taught me how to interview people as well as sharing a variety of skills related to personnel management. With his guidance, I learned how to write an internal newsletter that was distributed to all employees. I was making very little money, but I lived at the nurses' residence for ten dollars a week, including meals at the hospital. I learned a whole lot from Mr. Gagnon.

After about two years, and having sustained a broken heart at the hands of the Eli Lilly salesman, I began to think about finding another job closer to Boston. After a quick trip to the City for a job interview, a pharmacist friend of mine called and asked me to meet him for dinner in nearby Southbridge. I decided to join him.

On that fateful trip from Webster to Southbridge, there is a very long hill. As I came over the crest, I was hit head-on by a drunk driver who was passing a car and traveling in my lane. I recall recovering consciousness in what turned out to be the emergency room at Southbridge Hospital. I couldn't breathe. When I woke up again later, I learned that I looked fine when they brought me in by ambulance, but they learned quickly that I had a collapsed larynx and would need a tracheotomy. Fortunately, the surgeon on call that night had just headed out the door and a nurse went racing after him. He returned and saved my life.

When I awoke again during the early morning hours, I saw my brother Stan and Mr. Gagnon at the bottom of my bed. By morning, my parents had traveled from Maine and were now there too, concerned looks on their faces.

The car that I was driving that night was a snappy, navy blue Corvair. I loved it. My ever so clever father had been concerned because the engine was in the rear of that automobile, and he had filled the space under the hood with sandbags, primarily so that I would have better traction. When I was hit, the sandbags exploded upon impact, which saved my life. I had a broken kneecap, a broken finger, broken collarbone, chipped teeth damaged by the steering wheel, and now a trach that allowed me to breathe. That morning they x-rayed me from end to end and discovered that I had a hairline fracture in the second cervical of my neck. Suddenly that became the key issue; they had to stabilize me so that I wouldn't end up as a quadriplegic. My first communication was a note to my Mother. I asked: "Was it my fault?" She assured me that it wasn't and told me what had happened.

Not long after the x-rays, I was put in a body cast. This was the seventies and they didn't have a lot of technical expertise at that point. The cast began at the top of my head and went all the way to the bottom of my hips, forcing me to sit upright. The cast wrapped all around me. There were two armholes, and openings for my face and my ears. Under my chin, there was an opening for my trach, and one more opening at the very top of my head. Otherwise, the cast was solid all the way down my torso to stabilize me; I could not move my neck.

I returned home to Eliot via ambulance, knowing that I would be in that cast for at least 3 months. I lost weight. I went from a size 8 to a size 4. My mother made clothes to fit around my cast, and my now 32" waist. At the time of the accident, I had long auburn red hair, and my mother was concerned about that when they told her at the hospital that they were going to cut off. She told them, "NO." They pulled the hair up when putting on the cast, so it stuck out at the top. I have very fond memories of my dad, carefully washing my hair, strand by strand during those three months.

We also learned that "Humpty Dumpty" was unable to pull herself up in bed without help. My dad tied a strap to the opposing corner at the bottom of my bed which I could then use to pull myself upright. It was a learning experience for us all. My parents having launched me once, took me back home again and helped me heal. It took about a year for me to fully recover. I was fortunate to have that time with my parents. I was twenty-four years old and my mother died a mere five years later.

I had lessons to learn during my recovery, one of which was driving a car again. I had bought a new Mustang with the insurance money, and was tentatively beginning to drive with my father's help. However, I began having panic attacks. The fellow I had originally gone to see the night of the accident came to see me one weekend, and I remember one night we decided to go to a drive-in. He went for popcorn and returned to my side of the car to hand the popcorn to me. The door was locked and I could not physically get my hands and fingers to unlock it. I couldn't manage that. He got a key out and opened the door; I had three such attacks. Being a pharmacist though, my friend knew what was happening. He put his hand on my shoulder and told me that I would be ok.

Fearing that I might have other serious spinal complications, I returned to Southbridge Hospital again for a Myelogram, a shot of dye into the spinal cord. It turned out that was not the case. They gave me a prescription for the smallest dosage of Valium. I carried that plastic bottle around for three years and never once used them. They taught me the value of a crutch though. Occasionally, one needs one.

When the three months had passed, my parents took me back to Southbridge again, and they removed the cast and transitioned me into a metal neck brace for a few weeks. It was a relief, but I felt very strange as I maneuvered again without my protective shell.

As I began to feel stronger, I started thinking again about finding a job in the Boston area. One weekend, I found an advertisement for a sales representative position with a medical company named Hollister Incorporated, which was located in Chicago. The territory included Boston, Maine, northern New Hampshire, upstate Vermont, and Plattsburgh, New York. Since I was still not driving long distances, my parents drove me to Boston for the interview, and delivered me to the hotel door.

I interviewed with a wonderful gentleman and his wife, John and Minnie Schneider; who were probably in their mid-sixties. Hollister was a privately held company, with around four hundred employees. Mr. Schneider was the owner of the company. He had been a printer-craftsman in Chicago who bought the name Hollister, a name that was synonymous with birth certificates for babies in hospitals. I had a good interview with the Schneiders, and I was given some personality tests, which was common back then. I was not offered the position for the Boston territory, but they did offer me the same position in Pennsylvania. But since I wanted to stay close to home, I refused the offer.

A couple of months later I was visiting my college roommate in Bar Harbor when the phone rang; it was Hollister calling from Chicago. I was told that Mr. Schneider was going to be back in Boston and wanted to interview me again, seems the person whom they had hired for the Boston territory didn't work out. The woman on the phone calling from Chicago said: "Mr. Schneider would like you to wear your hair up for the interview." (How the times have changed.)

In retrospect, Mr. Schneider was absolutely old school— his philosophy was: **Only first class is good enough.** Products, People, Service were to be first class. At the time, I had long auburn hair, which Mr. Schneider told me was distracting. He counseled me by saying: "You are going to be selling to people and you don't want hair in your face." So I wore my hair up for the second interview. And after a time he said to me: "You can take your hair down now." He also told me in the interview: "You tested as a chief and I need some Indians," also a sign of the times. I wasn't certain at that point whether that was a positive or a negative. But time would tell.

It was obvious that Mrs. Schneider had warmed to me. We talked easily and I always felt that she cast the deciding vote that day. Finally after some deliberation, Mr. Schneider decided to take a chance and offered me the position in Boston. Life began again for me that day. With some trepidation, I accepted a position in a territory that involved thousands of miles of travel each year, as well as the driving chaos of downtown Boston. Though Mr. Schneider knew that I had been in an automobile accident, there was one small piece of information that I failed to tell him: I was just learning to drive again.

They gave me a company car, a Delta 88 Royale. I called it "The Blue Goose." A couple of years later, Mr. Schneider's sister drove a brand new Delta 88 Royal from the Hollister office in Chicago to my parent's driveway in Maine. It was a soft yellow and I named it "The Canary." Those cars were large and well-built. Once I became comfortable driving them, I felt very safe again behind the wheel. I had learned to drive again.

The position called for me to visit hospitals, surgeons, and retail accounts such as pharmacies and medical supply companies. My territory included the major hospitals in Boston from Mass General to Boston City Hospital, and all the others in between, as well as Maine and portions of the other New England states. I was always "on the road," and working for Hollister was one of the greatest adventures of my life. I had the opportunity to sell very high quality products for a company with an exceptional reputation. That fine reputation preceded me, but it was now in my hands.

With an excellent supervisor, Lei Barry, I learned the business, the nooks and crannies of each and every product. Though I never viewed myself as a salesperson, per se, I loved the products.... They were exceptionally well made and highly effective. I was very proud to be employed by Hollister, and my knowledge and enthusiasm was rewarded with successful sales. I was the very first sales person at Hollister who wrote over a million dollars in sales in one year, and I received recognition for that accomplishment. And from there, my career developed direction and velocity. I became a trainer in the field, then on to District Manager for the far Western states, Regional Manager for the Western half of the US, and finally Director of Sales for the Domestic Market.

Hollister began with high quality birth certificates, but Mr. Schneider was a genius at discovering needs in the medical field. Long before I had heard of Hollister, Mr. Schneider saw a vital need for patient identification, and pioneered the first system to clearly identify a patient. It started with newborns wearing colorful plastic beads on their wrists to identify them by name. However, the little bracelets that were held together by thin elastic bands often broke. When that happened, the baby's positive identity was lost. Mr. Schneider recognized this need and developed a soft plastic band with a strong Mylar lining that would not easily break. These bands were numerically correlated with one for the mother's wrist and two for the newborn. There was a paper insert with the name, and a closure on each band that made them secure until they were cut off with scissors. A positive patient identification system was born. Mr. Schneider pioneered patient identification in the world and his gift for recognizing needs in the medical industry led to many other unique products: Colostomy and Ileostomy pouches , wound care products, and so many others.

Just after I joined Hollister, I met my future husband,

though my father had known Rex Jenson for some time. He was an Airman stationed at Pease Air Force Base where they both worked. Rex was from California and was serving four years in the Air Force. My father thought he was a good guy, and Rex really liked my dad. One weekend, on a Saturday, the man I was dating at the time came over to the house to go sailing in our new sailboat. Though having owned several lobster boats, my father had no experience with sailboats, but somehow had just bought one. He discovered that Rex knew how to sail and invited him over to teach us.

Of course father neglected to tell me Rex was tall, good looking, and a contemporary of mine. He walked in the door and I remember saying to my dad later: "You could have told me this guy was my age." My dad had never brought anyone home from the base, unless they were fifty or sixty years old.

I have a photograph of that first so-called date on the Piscataqua River. My future husband was at the tiller, and the fellow I was dating was sitting next to me. As we were approaching the end of the sail, my dad motioned to Rex to land the shiny new boat at our dock. We were flying along and headed directly at my father who was standing at the end of the dock nervously awaiting our arrival. I could feel my blood pressure rising, as well as my dad's. I could hear him yelling at Rex, "Turn it, TURN IT"!

Well, Rex was a far better sailor than any of us, and he turned the boat just in time to smoothly cozy it up to the dock. Perfection. I had never seen anyone confront my dad in such a way, and as we were streaking toward the dock, I had decided that I would never see Rex Jenson again.

Rex and I married and enjoyed living near my parents and

spending a lot of time on the Piscataqua River together. However, within a few short years, my dear mother developed a brain tumor and died. I was devastated, and find it difficult to write those words even today. My mother was the ultimate driving force in my life. She taught me so much, and by example, showed me how one should live a good life. Her death left me with an abyss, which exists even now.

But Rex was in my life and I had a wonderful job to fall back on; my dad was healthy and coping with the changes in his life.

When I was promoted to District Manager, we moved to Los Angeles, California where I began a new role with Hollister. I made the transition, but found myself overwhelmed by the changes in my life. After several months of what probably should be termed "clinical depression," I decided to see a psychologist. The first appointment was a disappointment. I felt no connection with this man; we talked a little but I found it fruitless.

I decided to try one more meeting with him, and this time it turned out to be pivotal. The psychologist asked me what I thought were the reasons why I was so troubled. I listed my issues, with tears flowing. Finally, he stopped me and reiterated my words. He said: "You have lost your mother, you have moved 3000 miles from home, you have a new job with far greater responsibility, you developed an allergy to your two cats and left them behind in Maine with your father. You are trying to settle into a new home and have no friends living nearby. Yes? And just why, Andrea, do you think that you wouldn't be sad and suffering from this emotional upheaval?"

Once that doctor said those words to me, I realized that I had every reason to be unhappy and feel lost and out of control. He gave me PERMISSION. When I left his office I felt as though a massive weight had been lifted. I grew up in an era when consulting a psychologist or a psychiatrist was rarely discussed and often considered a weakness. However, that event made such a huge difference in my life, that I have on occasion related it to others who I saw suffering in a similar way. People have often perceived me as a very strong individual, a self-contained New Englander. My sharing this has perhaps helped others.

After a few years as a District Manager, I was offered the position of Regional Manager, covering about everything west of the Mississippi. I remained in the Los Angeles area for about five years.

One Friday, while working at home, I received a phone call from the corporate headquarters, and was offered the position of Director of Sales for the entire United States. I was stunned. Rex was comfortably employed by Security Pacific Bank, having finished his college degree program. I was in an MBA program at Loyola Marymount University, and closing in on getting my master's degree. Rex was willing to move and looked into opportunities in Chicago. He interviewed with two banks, got offers from both, and accepted a position with The First National Bank of Chicago.

On a trip back to Chicago to discuss this move, I visited the campus of Loyola University in downtown Chicago. They heard my story, and were willing to work with me, although the two Jesuit universities are not affiliated. I took the few required classes that I needed at Loyola in Chicago, transferred them, and eventually was awarded an MBA from Loyola Marymount. The degree in English was bedrock; the second degree in business proved a potent combination for me. They made my journey in management a comfortable path to follow.

Hollister was growing rapidly. Mr. Schneider stepped aside, chairing The Board of Directors, and made Michael C. Winn, who had previously been the company attorney, the new president. I now would be working with Mr. Winn, and had never had as much responsibility or people to manage before. It was a challenge unlike any other that I had faced.

The learning curve was steep, but gradually I settled in and became comfortable in the role as Director of Sales. After an especially good sales year, I found myself sitting next to Mr. Schneider at a banquet, knowing full well that he must have requested it. To my utter amazement, the man said to me: "I'm sorry I gave you such a hard time in the beginning. You have done well for us."

That's all he said—and I sat there thinking: "Did he really say that to me?" Those few words suddenly gave me a sense of freedom. I hadn't fully realized the cloud that I had been working under, feeling at times as though I was always on probation. But Mr. Schneider's words were a validation of my contribution to the company and his respect for me. This gentle, though tough Midwesterner, and a genius of a man, in a very few simply spoken words, made everything right.

Because Mr. Schneider had no children, he benevolently created a Trust, which eventually put the company into the hands of the employees. I could never have asked for a more challenging, enlightening and satisfying work experience than my time at Hollister.

In late 1985, I began considering my future plans. I was fatigued and felt that it was time for me to leave Hollister. I submitted my resignation in 1986. Mr. Winn was not happy when I announced that I was resigning, but what he did for me was insist that I retire instead of resign. At the time I really had no idea there would be a difference in the two. They gave me a party, and a lovely piece of sculpture that had been in my office, and said many kind words about my time with the company.

I left Hollister with both sadness and delight. I had been given an opportunity beyond my wildest dreams. And I have learned over the years about the extraordinary benefit of "retiring." Hollister management has continued to invite me to key events. Along with several other contemporaries, I represent an era in the growth of Hollister. They call us "Pioneer Retirees." Recently, I was invited to the Ninetieth Anniversary celebration, and I remembered that I had been in charge of the Sixtieth Anniversary celebration. When I started at Hollister there were around four hundred people working for the company. I was told recently that Hollister Incorporated now employs four thousand people worldwide.

After leaving Hollister, Rex and I decided to begin a new odyssey in life. When we telephoned Rex's parents and announced our decision to leave our jobs and travel for a few years, they initially told us it was a wonderful idea and they were delighted for us. However, within less than a half hour, the phone rang and they both loudly expressed their concerns.

What were we thinking? We were giving up the employment security that we had worked so hard to develop.

But Rex and I were not to be deterred. We both had dedicated ourselves to education and our work, and we needed a break. Rex left his position at the bank, we sold most everything including the condominium in Chicago, and we put a few things into storage. We bought a thirty-five foot aluminum Airstream motor home, towed a bright red Suzuki Samurai and travelled all over the United States and Canada. We had the opportunity to visit his family quite often on the West Coast and my father who was still living in Maine. Our "great escape" gave us some time to spend with my dad and Rex's parents before we lost them all. Winters were spent in Florida, primarily in the Keys, where we learned scuba diving. One winter we left the Airstream and flew off to Australia and New Zealand to do some diving, where both of us experienced the wonder of the Great Barrier Reef. We also traveled to Europe twice, circumnavigating the British Isles on one trip, and enjoying the Continent on another.

After four years of educational and play-filled travel, one day Rex announced that he was tired of being a "professional tourist." That started me thinking: "What are we going to do when we grow up ... again?" During our travels, I met a woman who told me about a federal agency called FEMA, the Federal Emergency Management Agency. She described it as an assistance program for those who had been hurt by a natural disaster such as a hurricane, tornado or flood. She told me that she was retired and was doing it part time. I was intrigued and went in search of information. Once back in

Maine, I wrote to Senator Edmund Muskie asking about contacting the agency, (This was before the Internet.) Within a short time, the Senator wrote back and provided an address. I then wrote to FEMA, and thus began our next twenty-year adventure.

Within a few weeks, our packages arrived and after completing the extensive application, having our fingerprints taken, we submitted a request to be considered as Disaster Assistance Employees (DAE's). After a few more weeks, we received notification that we had been accepted into the program. Time passed and we heard nothing, and continued on with our travels in the motorhome.

One day while visiting Rex's parents in California, we received a phone call from FEMA deploying us to assist after a tornado that struck in Alabama. We swiftly made plans to leave, and were aboard the airplane when Rex suddenly turned to me and said, "What is this anyway?" Not really having much of a clue either, I told him, "As far as I know, we don't have to stay if we don't like it." Little did I know that we were about to be inoculated with challenges beyond our wildest imagination. A new journey in life.

It was a small tornado in Alabama, and we found ourselves asking questions of those who had damages, and then filling out applications for their assistance. We enjoyed helping those who had been affected by the disaster, the FEMA staff were a group of kind and willing trainers, and both Rex and I felt good about the first calm and well-organized experience with the agency. However, months and months went by again, and we heard nothing further. In fact, we were so concerned that we made an appointment to see management at the

Regional Office in Atlanta to find out whether we were ever going to be deployed again. We met very briefly with a FEMA Manager who told us that we would be deployed in order, based on our last deployment. "That's how it works. You'll get your chance." We told the gentleman that we hoped to work sometime soon, and left there with little optimism that we would.

And then along came "ANDREW...."

Early on the morning of Aug. 24, 1992, a storm called "Andrew" slammed into the Florida coast, just south of Miami. It was a catastrophic Category 5 Hurricane, with wind speeds that were later estimated at more than 160 miles per hour; the gauges used to collect such data had been broken. The phone rang again and within seconds we were deployed to Miami. We were to report to the FEMA Disaster Field Office located in the vacant and dilapidated former Eastern Airlines building.

Rex and I were sent in different directions; he was immediately placed in the field meeting with Disaster Survivors. The next morning after my arrival, I boarded a large motorhome along with several others, and headed off around 4AM in the dark, and we were delivered to what remained of Florida City. During the first couple of days there, we worked outside in the sun and heat and wrote applications for those who suffered damages. When it rained, and it poured often, we escaped into what used to be a building and what was now a completely dark foundation with no windows or lighting. Who knew what else might have sought refuge there, and we all suspected that there were probably creepy-crawlies, snakes and mold and mildew. There we were in the sun and the rain, with nothing but a clipboard and a pen. By the third day we had a canopy overhead, but were still working in the rain and 90+ degree temperatures.

In addition to the difficult conditions, we often heard gunfire and soon discovered that there were heavily-armed U.S. Marshalls on the rooftops surrounding the area where we were located. There were looters. I recall thinking that this must be what it was like in a war zone.

On the fourth day in Florida City, the woman who was assigned to be in charge came unglued, and the next thing I knew I was in charge. Catapulted to a management position within a week. It was actually funny since at that stage, I knew more about the motorhome that was our transportation, than I did about FEMA. But I did know how to manage people. We did what we needed to do. My reign lasted only a couple of days and I was told to report to the Disaster Field Office in Miami, where I would be working in Individual Assistance.

I began my new job at the Disaster Field Office. My good fortune was the opportunity to work with the wonderful Suzy Honeywell. Sadly, she is no longer alive, but is fondly remembered by all who knew her. Suzy knew FEMA. She taught me how to work cases and how to get things done. This was before computers and everything was handwritten and put in files! Thousands and thousands of files. Somehow, Suzy could hand you cases that would take days to complete, and you found yourself thanking her! She was such a delight. One day she came to me and somehow made me feel like I was receiving a promotion. What she subsequently assigned to me were some of the more difficult cases that were pending. It didn't take long to discover that I had once again, been hoodwinked by "Suzy Q." However, the experience that I gained from those cases provided a vast education on the Stafford Act and FEMA policies and procedures. That baptism by fire launched my career with the Agency.

I was a rookie when I went to Miami, but after working some of the more complex cases for many months, I became fairly well known. I found myself working in "the corner office," reviewing news releases and the occasional speech, in addition to my case work.

After 8 months in Miami, I let a key FEMA Manager, to whom I was now reporting, know that I was leaving. He then told a couple of attorneys at FEMA Headquarters in Washington, DC, with whom I had worked, that I was returning home. He put them on the speakerphone, and to my amazement and pleasure they thanked me for the work that I had done. They said that I had helped FEMA with difficult and confusing cases, and through re-inspections and review, provided recommendations for the appropriate outcome. The initial experience and knowledge that I gained after Hurricane Andrew has stood me well all these years.

"People Support What They Help Create"

Somewhere along the way while employed by Hollister, I learned that phrase. It has consistently guided my concept and style of management, and my thinking, throughout my life and career. It quite possibly came from the great Peter Drucker, and his thoughts on management.

I learned long ago that people want to participate, they want to have a say about how to accomplish a task. They will share their ideas if they are made comfortable, and realize that their thoughts are valued. In graduate school and at Hollister I learned how to engage staff and encourage them to participate. At FEMA, I have often used those skills. I have been told that I am a good manager because I listen to others.

One of the most memorable experiences that I have had with FEMA happened after Hurricane Floyd, where I was assigned to head the Applicant Services Group in Raleigh, North Carolina. This group works directly with Disaster Survivors and assists them if they have questions or concerns about their application with the Agency. Unfortunately we had some unique issues at this disaster and there were more problems to resolve than usual.

I was in charge of a group of thirty people: I called them the "United Nations." We had staff from many different areas; they spoke several languages, were all different ages, and had different backgrounds. But this remarkable group became a powerful team that supported each other, provided exceptional service, understanding, and care to the Disaster Survivors. I learned a great deal from them.

A photograph was taken of the group toward the end of that deployment, and you could tell that everyone enjoyed and cherished the experience.

At that disaster I did something I never do. But it was the Holiday Season, and I was trying to think of something I could do to recognize their fine work before we went our separate ways. One evening I found myself in Restoration Hardware and discovered these tiny acorns; beautiful little pewter acorns with a magnet attached. I bought acorns for everyone, and the next day I got poster board and drew my interpretation of a sturdy oak tree (Okay, so maybe you needed some imagination there). When we had our morning meeting that day, I gave each of them my gift. I explained to them that we were all acorns on this tree, and we were able to accomplish such great things because of our unified strength.

I was never more proud of a group than this one. I still go to disasters, and someone who I may not immediately recognize, will come up and say to me: "I still have my acorn." I still have my acorn too.

Over the twenty years I have been with FEMA, I would estimate I have worked somewhere around forty disasters. In addition to Hurricane Andrew, I was deployed after the Loma Prieta Earthquake near San Francisco, the Midwest floods when the Mississippi overflowed, the four hurricanes that struck Florida one season, the epic damage from Katrina, and many more. I have viewed my time with FEMA as a very valuable experience in my life. I have given of myself, but have received a thousand-fold in return. I have seen the devastation from floods, earthquakes, tornados, and catastrophic hurricanes. But what I wasn't prepared for was the Terrorist Attack in New York City.

Epilogue

In The Absence of Buildings

Big cities have strong scents, smells from food, exhaust, the undercarriage of the city. But New York City now had an entirely different odor. It was dreadful, sickening, and permeated everything and everywhere you went. The city was eerily quiet, no horns blaring, few cars. And people were kind; went out of their way to hold open a door, ease someone into a line.

When 9/11 took place I was deployed to West Virginia, but I saw the horrific disaster on television. An equally stunned longtime friend and fellow FEMA employee asked me if I would go to New York City if requested. Without a thought, I answered yes; she said she didn't think she could do it. However, later that day she told me she would go if I went. I kept thinking that if my country ever needed me, it was now. We both went and worked together.

Within hours, I was contacted by the Atlanta office and asked to return home to Maine and prepare to deploy to New York City. I left West Virginia that day. Once home I rented a car locally; there were no airplanes in the sky. Rex helped me pack. There were hugs and tears. He often said he was never more proud of me than that day when I headed off alone into the unknown. When it's a hurricane, tornado, earthquake or flood, you have a pretty good idea of what you will find, but that was not the case this time.

Initially I was assigned to the FEMA Center near Ground Zero. One could barely breathe. And didn't want to. It was far too small a space to accommodate those seeking help. It was deafening—you could not think. Everyone seemed to be speaking at once and in a different language; it captured the definition of pandemonium, with sadness and sorrow everywhere you turned.

When public transportation began to move, I took the subway to work; people were polite, quiet, and separate in their thoughts. In a week and a half I was transferred to a new

FEMA center at Pier 94. Riding there the first day, I found I was studying the skyline; I felt a immense weight of sadness from the absence of those two towering buildings. That sadness remains to this day.

The Pier 94 location had the same long lines and its own share of chaos. Every morning for four months I walked from Times Square to Pier 94; FEMA provided a bus, but I needed the mile walk to sort things out. I had been given the role of Assistant Manager at the FEMA Disaster Assistance Service Center.

The terrorist attacks of 9/11 left an indelible mark on me as it did on all Americans. I was proud to serve with FEMA in New York City. Without hesitation I would do it again. In a very small way we reached out a hand to help our country heal.

As life and times go, I have sometimes walked a crooked path. The one absolute, my family and friends have always been there with support, love, and guidance.

Hollister convinced me that "Only First Class" is good enough, and how important it is to do things well. FEMA tossed me into the trenches, where I learned to expect the unexpected. Together they taught me the value of both.

Jon Hlafter

University architect (retired), family man

I am a second generation American. My mother's father came to this country from the Austro-Hungarian Empire. He was born in what is now Hungary, but he and my other grandparents were Slovak. He left his home when he was about eighteen and came to America, where he worked in the coal mines of Eastern Pennsylvania until he contracted Black Lung Disease. Having learned to butcher animals while in Europe, he moved to New Jersey and opened a butcher shop. He then married Anna, a young Slovak woman who died when their child, my mother, was just three years old. To help care for his young daughter, my grandfather wrote to his in-laws back in Europe and said: Anna has died, send Ilona. So Ilona, the younger sister, was called in from the field where she was tending the cows. Her belongings were packed up in a trunk (which I now own) and she was sent off to America to marry my grandfather. Baba, the person that I knew as my grandmother, was really my great aunt. She and my grandfather ran the butcher shop/grocery store through the Depression, World War II and beyond, supporting themselves, my mother and two younger siblings.

As a young child, my mother was ill with scarlet fever. She later became self-conscious about a scar on her eye that was caused by the disease. Although she was sent to secretarial school to learn typing (apparently she was very skilled), she was uncomfortable facing people, given what she thought was her glaring abnormality. After leaving school, she went to work in local woolen mills, where the loud machinery damaged her sensitive hearing. (Mom and I both had to wear hearing aids later in life.) My father also had a difficult childhood, but for different reasons. His father used to beat him and lock him in a dark closet for hours. Growing up in those days was not easy.

My father was an excellent athlete. (I still remember going to watch him play softball when he was in his late 40's.) As a young man he had been scheduled for a tryout with the Chicago Cubs, but he broke his leg, so the tryout never happened. He had been a good football player in high school, but his father wanted him to work on Saturdays and bring in money to the family. Somehow it worked out that he practiced with the team and played on Saturdays anyway, without telling his father. It ended with my grandfather going to the principal and having Dad expelled. He never went back. Neither my father nor my mother ever earned a high school diploma. I do think there were some pretty good genes, but they didn't have a chance to develop.

My father and mother were married in 1938, when they both were in their thirties. They had met in a social club for Slovak Lutherans. Mom once told me that earlier she had been going with a German man who went on to become a lawyer, but my grandfather disapproved of her marrying outside of the Slovak community.

I am an only child. My father and mother wanted me to have all the things they didn't have. As a result, Mom expected me to be absolutely perfect in my studies at school.

In elementary school, I don't remember that I ever received an academic grade below an Excellent. I do remember that in high school the first mark I received below an A (in junior year, in Physics) was a B+. That was a major disappointment for my mother—and me.

My father worked in a factory that manufactured ball bearings. He was an inspector who made sure that everything on the line was just right. One of the most difficult times I had with my father was when he taught me how to drive. He insisted that I had to do things in just the right way—his way. I didn't think either of us would get through the ordeal.

I grew up in Raritan, New Jersey (a few miles north of Princeton) and went to Somerville High School. We were a church-going family— good Slovak Lutherans. I went to Sunday School, attended Confirmation classes, joined the youth group—the whole deal. The 1950's were a great time to be in high school. Almost always, both in high school and earlier in elementary school, there were more smart girls than boys, so if a boy was at or near the top of the class, it was easier to be singled out. I was the one who became the Student Council President.

My high school guidance counselor saw that I was good in math and could draw. She recommended that I become an engineer or an architect. In those days, if someone in authority recommended that you do something, you did it. So I applied only to four universities that had schools of architecture. My guidance counselor specifically advised that I should apply to Princeton, where I was accepted with a scholarship. Just a couple of years ago, a Princeton alumnus from the Class of 1941 came up to me at a meeting. The name "John Scott" was on his name tag. He asked: "Do you know me?" I said: "The name sounds familiar but I don't think so." He said: "My sister was Eleanor Scott—do you remember her?" She was my guidance counselor. Apparently she and her brother had conversations about me, and they were both delighted when I was accepted at Princeton. It turned out that Scott was only the second person from Somerville High that was accepted at Princeton. I was third or fourth. Of course, Princeton changed my life.

I am a member of the Class of 1961 . My class was the first at Princeton to have more high school students than prep school students; it was a real watershed. For the most part, my friends tended to be from high schools; but one of my roommates was a graduate of the Choate School and came from a very different background. I found it rather easy to be part of Princeton, probably because I never aspired to join one of the more prestigious clubs. I did join Quadrangle Club, which was made up of mostly straight-arrow, middle-of-the-road students. Some very fine people had been members, including both Princeton President Robert Goheen '40 as well as Harvard President Neil Rudenstein '56. Most members of my class clearly had more money than I had (or would ever have), but that fact did not cause me much soul searching.

I majored in Architecture as an undergraduate and stayed on for two more years as a graduate student to obtain a professional degree. Princeton then had a six- year program that was rather unusual. Most public universities have traditionally had a five-year program, leading to Bachelor of Architecture degree. Harvard and Yale will accept students after they have received their Bachelor of Arts degree and will grant a Master of Architecture degree after three years. By staying at Princeton for a total of six years, I was awarded an uncommon professional degree: Master of Fine Arts in Architecture.

I received scholarships to finance most of my expenses during those six years. My parents were able to cover other costs, my mother having taken a job in an elementary school lunchroom. Mom was not especially happy that I chose architecture. She wanted me to be a doctor or a Lutheran minister. I'm not sure what my father would have had me do; he worked nights for much of the time when I was growing up, so I never developed a relationship with him that was as close as my relationship with my mother.

I met my wife Pat when I was in Graduate School and she was a student at the Westminster Choir College. The University was an all-male institution in those days, but Lutheran students could invite female students from other colleges to fellowship meetings. More than one happy marriage developed. Religious life played a more important role in campus life then than it does today. Undergraduates had to attend Chapel when I arrived in 1957 but I could fulfill the requirements by attending services in town at the Lutheran Church of the Messiah. Pat and I are still members there today.

Pat and I were married in 1965 and within the year moved to Massachusetts, where I did my professional internship and fulfilled my draft obligation with the Massachusetts Air National Guard, first at Logan Airport in Boston and later at Otis Air Force Base on Cape Cod . We enjoyed the excitement of seeing new places and meeting new friends. After having worked for Bell Telephone in Pennsylvania, Pat went to work for New England Bell. I joined a very small architectural firm in downtown Boston. Both of the partners were Harvard alumni. One was a descendant of John Adams. (Adams once said that he had to study war and diplomacy so his children and grandchildren could study many other things—-including architecture. At least one did!) We lived in Newton Corner, just beyond the Boston line, in a brick saltbox townhouse on a thin sliver of land between a main railroad line and the Charles River, just across from a beautiful Gothic tower in Watertown. The monthly rent was $125.00. We enjoyed going to movies at the Brattle Theatre in Cambridge and having pizza at the College Inn on Mass Avenue. It was fun.

One day I received a call from an architect friend who had been offered a position in the Planning Office at Princeton. He had just opened his own office and recommended me for the position instead. I did get a call from the University and decided to accept an offer to work there for what I thought would be about five years, planning for the implementation of coeducation. That was in 1968. I ended up working there for over 40 years.

My father died in 1970, when our daughter Meredith was just about a year old. I had given my parents tickets to see the New York Knickerbockers play in Madison Square Garden at the Christmas Festival. They drove to Princeton (because we were then living in University housing) and went on to New York by train. Late Christmas night, we received a call from Mom saying that Dad had suffered a heart attack. After getting off the return train at Princeton Junction on the southbound side, they became confused, and went to the northbound side. Then, seeing the "Dinky" arrive on the southbound side, Dad ran through the tunnel and up the stairs, where he had a heart attack and died.

Because my mother had a severe hearing problem, she was frightened by living alone. When my father died, she came to live with us for almost 20 years. She died when Meredith was a junior in college. "Grammy" was our built-in baby sitter. Jon and Meredith would go into Grammy's room to read stories and have fun. Both would commonly wish her goodnight before they went to bed. I break up when I talk about it, but in his college application essay, Jon wrote about his not stopping by on the night his grandmother died.

Both of our children attended local Princeton schools and Princeton University. We became unhappy with the public system when Meredith was in junior high. She had gone on a trip to a state park, and a fool teacher left her alone in the woods. She had to be found by a park ranger. The teacher in question was eventually dismissed. (Patty has said it was the one time in our marriage when she thought I was going to punch somebody out. I was furious.) After that awful experience, we took Meredith out of the public system and sent her to all-girl Stuart Country Day for her four years of high school. Jon stayed in the public school system and graduated from Princeton High. Meredith applied for Early Action only at Princeton. Jon applied elsewhere but decided that Princeton was the place for him as well . He sang with the TigerTones, the singing group that also provided his circle of friendships. He is now an attorney with a large New York law firm. His wife, Claudia Hamilton, is currently in training to become a Montessori teacher. Meredith is the Director of Global Sanctions Compliance at American Express, also in New York. She is married to Kelly Terrell, a high school teacher and drama coach; they have two children, Julia Grace and Emma.

Coeducation at Princeton was approved in 1969. There is a kind of nostalgia among some alumni for the all-male Princeton. I do feel some of that nostalgia, but it is a better university now, flat out. Harvard is a bigger institution with fine graduate schools, but for an undergraduate education, I don't think there is a better place than Princeton. The women who fifty years ago might have attended schools like Bryn Mawr or Mount Holyoke are now attending Princeton. They help create a better environment for learning. As a result, I believe that the demands made on students today are greater than they were when I was a student.

Princeton has changed in other ways, as a story that was told to me can illustrate. When my mother lived with us, she suffered from rheumatoid arthritis. She required a series of orthopedic operations— two hips, two knees— and was in the hospital many times. One evening, when I had gone to visit her at the hospital, a nurse came into the room and I had to step into the corridor. I discovered that the patient in the very next room was Douglas Brown, then retired, having served for decades as the Dean of the Faculty and the first Provost at Princeton. He knew that I had gone to Somerville High School and told me that he had been the first student from Somerville to be accepted at Princeton many years before. He went on to explain that while in high school he had earned money by sweeping floors in one of the local mills with a fellow student, Paul Robeson. Robeson's father was then the minister at the Presbyterian Church on Witherspoon Street in Princeton. At that time, New Jersey had a kind of Mason-Dixon line. While high Schools from Somerville north were integrated, the high schools from Princeton south were segregated. Robeson's father wanted his son to go to an integrated school, so Paul was sent to Somerville High, where he became friendly with Brown. They both applied to Princeton. Brown was accepted, Paul Robeson was not. He went to Rutgers instead. The rest of the story is well-known. Today, I have no doubt that both would have been accepted by a much different Princeton.

For most of my years at Princeton I served as the Director of Physical Planning and, ultimately, as the University Architect, reporting to the Vice President for Facilities. My job was to plan and implement projects to meet the physical needs of the University. At first, before I received my professional license, my title was Assistant to the Director of Physical Planning and I was mostly involved in the programming of projects that were under consideration. About two years after my arrival, the Director was asked to leave. By that time, I had been granted my license and was put in charge of the office. I was 31.

My expanded responsibilities included having to make presentations of proposed projects to various boards and committees. Always wary of making off-the-cuff remarks, I began to make a point of writing everything down first in preparation for a talk. I also did my best to be rather cautious in conversations with University Officers and Trustees. Although my most sensitive task was to recommend new projects to the Grounds and Buildings Committee of the Board, the daily interactions with faculty and administrators kept me very busy. At Princeton, it is the responsibility of the President, the Provost and their advisors to match potential needs and potential resources, so a proposed project can be funded and approved. The Administration counted on me and my colleagues in Facilities to provide accurate information regarding the scope and cost of a project, very often **before** we could possibly know all the pertinent facts. Most often, the final cost exceeded our initial estimates, given more information and changing requirements. Nonetheless, it was our responsibility to implement each approved project's scope within an approved project budget. Of course, the time I spent with architects on the actual design of the projects was always more fun for me than estimating their costs.

For me the joy of working at Princeton was two-fold: I enjoyed the beauty of the place and the contacts with people I met there. Just walking through the campus was and is a source of pleasure and renewal , although in retirement I inevitably come across things that might have been done better under my watch. I especially valued (and usually enjoyed) my contacts with very bright, intelligent people: administrators, faculty and staff, trying to make Princeton a better place—- as well as consultants that we hired for the same purpose.

While at the University I had the privilege of serving four presidents, Robert Goheen, William Bowen, Harold Shapiro and Shirley Tilghman. Clearly, all were kind and supportive, but what struck me most was their good sense. They were the ultimate decision-makers, the true builders. My role was to be a good steward in their service.

At my retirement party, an elegantly bound volume was presented to me that featured photographs of projects on which I had worked, along with letters from the architects, like Robert Venturi, whose buildings, both on our campus and elsewhere, I regard as very special. I feel very indebted to the several staff members in Facilities and in other University offices who were responsible for producing the book. I do like to look at the pictures, but I am embarrassed by the generous sentiments expressed in the letters.

In retirement, I have often asked myself whether those years of service to Princeton actually resulted in any truly special contributions of my own. I would like to think that the honest answer has something to do with the University achieving an understandable transition from a place of architectural memories to a place of architectural aspirations. Did my low profile attempts to do the right thing serve as a vehicle for progress by others? Was I lucky enough to be in the right place at the right time?

Of course, the important questions of my retirement should not focus on what was but on what is and can be. Will I ever be able to do a competent watercolor again? What contributions can I still make?

Terri Gregg

First college grad, linguist, proud wife and mother, Mafia DNA

My maternal great grandparents came from Italy in the late 1800s and settled in Amsterdam, New York, west of Albany. The family name on my maternal side was Morreale. My paternal great grandparents also came from Italy and settled in New York City. That family name was Curro. My grandparents were born in America in the early 1900s; my paternal grandfather moved my dad and his family to Albany to get away from the Mafia family that had settled in New York City. By the time my parents were born there seemed to be no Mafia problem. My Dad's family ended up in Albany. My Mom's family, half Italian (and half Polish), stayed in Amsterdam.

Up to my early twenties, we would go to Amsterdam every weekend for big Italian family gatherings, until the grandparents passed on. My grandfather on my mother's side had worked for labor unions. I remember the house in Amsterdam was rundown, dilapidated; if you broke through the floors you weren't surprised. They had no money to speak of. We had no money; we made do with what we had. My grandfather on my mother's side used to tell me he would steal food from the meat factories and from the butcher. On my Dad's side, I don't think they were that poor, but they owned a very old home in Albany.

I was born in Troy, New York. My family lived in

Watervliet in an apartment, across the Hudson River from Troy. My father, raised in Albany, went to Korea for three years, and worked for Bell Telephone when he returned. He worked on communications and power lines when he worked, but they were on strike a lot of the time. My Mom had to temp when that happened, any job she could get. There were four kids, two boys, two girls (I am the oldest of four). My parents eventually moved us into an old house from the apartment. The things I remember the most were bad things (maybe good things). In retrospect they weren't so bad. I recall my Dad coming in after work; he would have money in his hand and envelopes spread out on the table. He would put five dollars in each of four or five envelopes. Every week he would do that. One would be for clothing, one for heat, one for food, one for miscellaneous. That's how we lived, paycheck to paycheck. And when he didn't work, my Mom would have to temp.

Back then when I was seven or eight, I thought all that was awful; I was so embarrassed. My friends didn't live like that. If they wanted to go out and buy something, they went out and bought something. While my friends went out for dinner, we were picking foods from our garden, berries from the plants in the yard, fruit from the trees in the backyard, and went fishing for trout which my dad filleted for dinner and hunting for deer which produced enough venison for my family. My friends came to school in pretty dresses, in nice cars. My Dad had an old Delta 88 for twenty five years, changed the oil, did everything to it, the only car we ever owned! Six of us in the car all the time. But we were a tight knit family, even though my parents fought a lot over stupid things, bumping heads, my mother being half Polish half Italian, my Dad full blooded

Italian. One time my Dad flipped the table over and said: "I can't do this anymore," and out he went. He came back, but it is amazing how those little ordeals remain with you forever.

I loved my Dad, and my Mom, but I think I had a better relationship with my Dad. That's still true; they are 80 and 76 respectively, and live in a two bedroom townhome in Vorheesville, ten miles from Albany. As my Mother says, "It's a gift beyond my wildest expectations." They lived in the Watervliet home forever, and when they finally sold it they made a profit of $100,000, used it to buy the townhome, which was filled with beautiful furniture by the former owner. My Dad received a golden parachute from Bell and my Mom did secretarial work until she was 62 or 63.

They won't accept help; my Dad says please don't. They still bump heads, but they are two Italian Catholics who don't believe in divorce, and they go to church every day, together. Communion every day, fish on Friday, the whole deal. In fact, we still do that with our kids, fish on Friday, especially during Lent. I have three kids and they love to visit their grandparents.

Watervliet was a tiny 8000 or so community when I was growing up, very gossipy. Consequently we were private. We had my father's brother and family living right down the street, and my aunt thrived on gossip. You couldn't say things to my aunt or cousins. But I remember, like it was yesterday, my Mom walking through the house with her Rosary beads praying the Rosary Novena; we would be kicked outside to play hide and seek with our friends. No car to go anywhere (Dad took it to work), and we never missed church on

Sundays or a Holy Day. That was my pre-teen life. I knew something was different with us. I felt we were hiding things all the time.

By the time I was a teenager I thought my parents were the worst in the world. Look at how much we're missing; my friends can go anywhere they want; they have all this money. Yet I was always taught from the beginning that money was not important. My husband will say to this day, "I don't care about money, but somehow it always follows me." We had 90 kids in my high school class, almost 400 in the high school. I wasn't especially popular, just normal. I was a cheerleader for football and basketball; I played on the boys tennis team (they cut the girls team out of the budget cause the school couldn't afford it).

My Dad discouraged college, not studying, but college. My Mother was saying, "Always strive to do your best." I was a good student; I liked to study—I graduated number four in my class and had an easy time with foreign languages. They offered Russian in my high school because our community was half Italian, half Russian Orthodox. I won a New York State Russian Scholarship to college. That was the only reason I could go because my parents had no money to send me.

I got into the University of Albany with the scholarship. All my professors in my Russian major were from Russia. It had the third best Russian program in the nation. In fact, my professor Sophia Lubensky is the author of a Random House Russian-English Dictionary of Idioms; she was amazing. I was only paying $1200 a year for college. I worked my way through, and of course I had to major in Russian to keep the scholarship: language courses, writing courses, reading courses. I minored in Political Science. I lived at home my first two years, so really I was paying $900 my first two years. The third and fourth years I lived off campus. But I was granted an RA position as a senior, so as a senior I didn't have to pay for room and board.

My dad still insisted that I should have not gone to college. He said, "I didn't want you to go to college, I wanted you to go to work at the bank; I know people down there. You could have been a teller. You could have made a great living down there." He was so negative. My mother? I don't know. She was still protective of our family name. She said, "Don't you go and sleep with anybody; I'll find out." Was I just flapping my wings? She wanted to have me under her thumb. Nevertheless, I know she was proud; she wanted me to do something different from what she did. I was the first person on both sides, parents, grandparents, cousins, uncles, aunts, who went to college and graduated. It was easier for my sisters and brothers; I had broken the ice. My sister became a nurse, and my brother a civil engineer, and the other brother a teacher. We all did it on our own. Some had to borrow money but they paid it back; I paid back $7000. For me it was tugging and pulling to get out of the nest to go to a nearby college, even with a scholarship.

Finally I was out of the house, and I was having a great time at college, the best time I ever had. Mainly, I didn't have to answer to my parents. I had a curfew in 12th grade; no more curfews when I was on my own. I wasn't a party girl, although I had a lot of boyfriends, but I was careful who I dated. I remember meeting one boy who invited me over to do marijuana and I never went over because I didn't want to have anything to do with that. A Jewish boy took me to New York City to meet his parents, but they simply left the room when they realized I wasn't Jewish. I dated many boys but was very careful and not looking to get serious until I had accomplished what I had to do for myself as far as studying.

The first two years were tough because I took my Dad's car to college and had to have it back so he could do the night shift at work when he was working. But I graduated with a 3.54 grade point average and a Summa Cum Laude. I put some feelers out. I was going to apply for the FBI, the CIA, government jobs in New York City. Then I had a rude awakening. My Dad called me in one day and said, "You can't apply to the FBI, or the CIA. We have Mafia ties; they will see that history." Of course I didn't believe that would happen, but sure enough, we had a family history that wasn't a good one.

I turned to my minor in Political Science and started looking for jobs in the government affairs arena. I got my first job in Albany as a lobbyist with a Trade Association, both foreign and domestic trade. I would review the trade regulations, learn them by heart, and see which Bills were coming up in Congress and The Senate and work on them. I was doing mostly research at the time. We had clients who paid to belong and paid us to represent them. I wasn't actually pacing the floor doing the lobbying. That was done later in Washington.

I had that job for only a couple of years. Then I met my husband; he was doing a post-doctorate in Albany for the New York State Department of Health. I met him at a picnic given by a mutual friend. He had gone to Georgetown, did his doctorate in Biology and Chemistry. He was raised in Troy, New York, and yet I had never met him until I was 25 and he was 30. He was raised in a family that was better off than my family. His father had gone to college for two years. He was the independent, wild child in the family; he juggled for attention with two siblings. He went to Catholic school from kindergarten through high school, went to Brockport State College (a SUNY school) and failed out his first year, came back to Troy (his father had died that year) and enrolled in a community college. He worked in a grocery store warehouse for two years and said: this is not for me.

He went down to Georgetown with his tail between his legs, to Washington, and said to Admissions: "If you let me go here I'll pull a 4.0 for you every year; I have no money." The man looked at him, looked at his credits from the community college and said: "OK, but if you pull a 3.9, you're out." He went as a sophomore, a transfer student, and ended with a Doctorate. He had gotten into medical and dental school, and thinks he should have gone to one of them, since by that time his concentration was Regulatory Affairs, and he could have used a medical degree.

When I met him I was dating boys, but he was different—he knew what he wanted to do with his life; he was a go-getter. For some reason that was the attraction. Since he was 30, my Mom asked me if he had been married; that was her first question. The answer was no. He was a studious person—to this day I can say he's not a socialite. He is conscientious and always has been. He says to our kids: "Study first, play later." I tell them the opposite: "Balance yourself, have a good time." We bump heads there a little bit. We got married a year and a half after we met; we did not live together during that year and a half. I would never do that to my parents. I had too much respect for them to do anything like that. Not that it's a bad thing, but we were told you don't do it.

I had taken the LSAT and was accepted at Albany Law School but my husband asked me to marry him and told me he was going back to Washington. Having done his post Doc, he was offered a job in Regulatory and Clinical Affairs with a Beltway Bandit, one of those companies that feeds off the FDA. I still intended going to law school, but when I looked in the newspaper, there were all these jobs in Washington offered for lobbyists. So I put that on hold, and was offered a lobbying position at the first company I interviewed with, because of the work I had done in New York State, same work, this time for a trade association representing chemical manufacturers.

I was on my feet lobbying through the halls of Congress more than I was in the office. It was a fantastic job; I loved it. I met all these people. There they were: Ronald Reagan, Ted Kennedy, they're all there. I said to my husband who wanted kids: "I got my degree; I want to work," so it was seven years before we had our first child. I held him off for five years and then I had trouble getting pregnant for two years. Then bam, bam, bam, three kids in five years. After our first child I went cold turkey on work. I had been on Capitol Hill at three in the morning waiting for a bill to be voted on; I didn't want to do that to a baby. My husband had been proud of what I was doing, and of course I was bringing in money, but it had to stop. Then I started doing interior design, which also brought in money.

Either you have it or you don't with interior design. My mother had taught me how to sew, so a neighbor would say: can you sew me some curtains, and then, can you sew me a cushion. All of a sudden here's your list of people who want things. So I developed my own business with interior design which allowed me to stay home with the kids, but at the same time feel I was contributing.

My husband had gone to the FDA and we were living in Northern Virginia, in a rental house at first, and then we saved enough money to buy a house inside the Beltway, which was going to help us out eventually when we sold the house. He wasn't making a ton of money but we were having a good time; we travelled. And then he was hired by Pharmacia Diagnostics, a private company in Maryland. He had been assigned to them, to approve their products, by the FDA, and he was getting those products approved quickly. They said: if you can do this at FDA, we'll hire you and pay you a lot more money. So we moved to Maryland, right outside of Baltimore. It was a wonderful place to live; I loved it. I'd move back there in a heartbeat. My eldest was two and my second was a newborn when we moved, but two months later Pharmacia told us they were shutting their doors in a year. Apparently they just wanted to clear up all the products that needed to be regulated.

My husband started hustling again and Johnson & Johnson hired him as Manager of Regulatory and Clinical Affairs at Ortho Diagnostics, in Somerville, New Jersey.

We moved up there; of course it was a corporate move (both Pharmacia, and then J & J, helped us out, the moves, closing costs, points and all that). So we were able to buy a really nice house, a beautiful house. Bob worked for J & J for seven years.

In his seventh year, Johnson and Johnson spun off some companies that were not doing well, and my husband was fortunate enough to receive a job offer from Roche Diagnostics in New Jersey. So Roche hired him; he had the FDA contacts and was getting approvals faster than anyone else in the country. He knew the regulations like the back of his hand, and he's one of the smartest people I've ever met.

A year and a half later, one of my girlfriends called me and told me Roche was closing the diagnostics company on Route 202 in New Jersey where Bob worked. I couldn't believe it. I dialed my husband; he said "I didn't hear that." He hung up, then he called me back: "Oh boy, that is true." Roche was acquiring Boehringer Mannheim in Indianapolis, Indiana and they had the better facility, so out we went to Indiana. We were told: you come with us you have a job, you don't come with us you don't have a job. Roche had done this so quickly we had to go out. We had to sell the house. Roche arranged the sale, moved us, again a corporate move. My husband dragged me kicking and screaming from New Jersey, kids four, six, and eight. We ended up in a school district that was number one in the State of Indiana: Carmel, Indiana, right above Indianapolis.

There we were in the Midwest, coming off a very aggressive East Coast, bumping into grocery carts and people saying: sorry I'm in your way (I didn't know where I was!). People were down to earth; they were friendly, non-aggressive, they would bend over backwards for you.

Priorities were God and family, and then everything else. I thought to myself, what a great place to raise a family; lucky them being born in the Midwest. But after seven and a half years I missed my family so much; we were missing out on holidays, birthdays, and simple weekend visits due to snow storms, distance and being 18 hours from New York.

I was still doing the interior decorating, doing fabulously working for a decorating center. Loved it, worked part time, only 24 hours, and by this time my husband was a Director of Regulatory and Clinical Affairs, which he has carried right up to today. He was making less than $200,000, but in Indiana $200,000 was like a million back on the East Coast. $500,000 was the cost of our first house and it was 7500 square feet. Very small lots, nice neighborhood. We bought a large house because I was hoping lots of family would visit; that never happened. My parents did come once in a while. I wasn't a person who wanted to show the world how successful we were. My husband doesn't want the world to think he's the richest person in the world, but he wants the world to know he's successful. He measures success by the number of products approved, company profits related to what he does. In Indiana everyone had a big house, or so it seemed, and we made a boatload of money when we sold the house in New Jersey that first time; we needed write-offs. Seven and a half years later we sold in Indiana and made a profit again.

Our first son started Catholic high school in Indiana; he went a year there. Bob was getting many job offers and he knew I wanted to get back to the East Coast. However, job offers came mostly from Texas and California. Then he got the call from Perkin Elmer in Boston, same position more money, corporate move, two and a half hours from Albany. It was ideal, but I suddenly had mixed emotions; I thought at the time that Indiana was a great place to raise kids.

We moved to Holliston, Massachusetts, 28 miles west of Boston, next to Hopkinton, where they start the Boston Marathon. We came down to 3900 square feet, still a big house. My oldest had a really rough time; he was bullied. In Indiana they had programs incorporated into the academics from Kindergarten to fifth grade called Everybody Counts. The programs taught students not to bully each other because a certain student may have a learning, mental, or physical disability which is something they cannot help. Moving to the Boston area was a culture shock for my kids because there was a lot of bullying. My oldest wore an Indianapolis Colts shirt to school one day; I told him not to do that because of the rivalry between the two teams, but he did it anyway. He paid for that. He was entering tenth grade and became reclusive; even though he was an athlete. He cried for the first two months in Massachusetts; not an easy time for him. I had him in to see the Guidance Counselor. The Principal said he realized the move was hard but our son would have to get used to it. For the five years we lived in that area I never got used to it; it was the absolute worst place we ever lived. There's an air that New Englanders have; either you fit in or you don't fit in. We never fit in.

I am not an enabling parent; I figured our son would have to deal with this on his own. I always figured adversity would make him stronger, and it did. From the first day in Massachusetts he vowed he would go back to Indiana, and he did. He was accepted to Purdue University and became more excited than I had ever seen him. When we lived in Indiana, he and my husband would go up to the Purdue games. All my son said for three years was "I'm going back." And he did. There was a lot of tight-knittedness, camaraderie in Indiana because there was nothing else to do there, so you would go to the games, and everyone rooted for the same teams. We would go to the Colts games all the time. If it was up to my husband we would still be there, and I know that about him. I would be there too if it weren't for my family.

Once I got off my mighty high horse I realized family was important; maybe I learned that in Indiana. Every child goes through the stage where they know way more than their parents, and because I went to college I was convinced I knew way more than my parents. I love my sister and my brothers. They don't visit each other; I'm the one who sends the cards, will go visit whenever I can. I will make sure my kids know their cousins. I was always away, so it's easier for me to pull everyone together. When you mature enough and realize your parents are good people (and so what if they fight and argue), you see they had their priorities in order. Then I discover those are my priorities.

One day my husband came in and said "How would you like to go back to New Jersey," and I started packing that night. I could not wait because I had friends and acquaintances here and no one had moved; after all, we had been in New Jersey a long time.

So here I am; I'm with my friends every day; they're good people. We have lunch, we get together. There are times when

I think I should be more reclusive; there's a time for everything. A well rounded person is the one who is going to fare the best. I'm in between.

My husband was offered a job with OraSure Technologies, their subsidiary that was working on a product he had been involved in way back when, an over the counter HIV test kit. They made an offer to my husband that was one he could not refuse. The test kit my husband is working on will hopefully impact the spread of AIDs as it will offer confidential advice for those who will be able to privately test themselves for the AIDs disease. The test can be done in the privacy of the home. HIV is still a major concern. Our country has come up with a cocktail to prolong life, but third world countries have not; this device is something that will, in the long run, help the world.

When first back in New Jersey, we rented a home because we hadn't sold in Massachusetts (the market was tumbling), and we had to be registered residents in New Jersey for our youngest son to attend North Hunterdon High School, in Annandale. He joined the football team and was doing a great job, 6' 5", almost 200 pounds, but he was told by the team if he didn't do cocaine or heroin with them, they were going to get him. It was his junior year; he came home, and like his big brother, he shut himself in his room, wouldn't tell me what was going on. He finally told a psychologist I took him to—by this time it was March. I went to the assistant principal at his school. She said she wanted me to talk to the drug czar. The drug czar said "I don't believe you; I don't believe he's not doing it with the kids" I said "I already had him tested and he came out negative." He said "I can't do anything unless you give me names." I said "You mean you can't tell me you do random drug testing?" He was silent. Needless to say he was fired at the end of the year. I took my son out of that school and put him in Somerville High School for his senior year. This would be the third high school he would attend in four years.

Our oldest son is very excited about a possible career in Computer Design and Engineering. Our second son started out in PreMed, and is currently considering which field of medicine interests him the most. Our third son is completing his first year at George Mason University. He doesn't know what he wants to be when he grows up.

My husband works all the time, weekends. He's never been unemployed. He's already saved for our retirement. We bought a beautiful house. I thank God every day for always giving us a wonderful life with all the twists and turns we have experienced; this is where he wanted us. He has been good to us and we are very thankful. Looking back, my life has blossomed from a simple humble one to one that is filled with excitement, health, peace and love.

Taylor Allen

Designer, builder, restorer of boats; wooden boat specialist; boatyard and family man

My parents moved with four of us from the Worcester area: Holden, Massachusetts to Rockport, Maine, in 1962, two sons and two daughters. My father had always wanted to do something in the boat business. He had been in submarines during World War II, stationed for part of the time in Alaska (I think his ideal move would have been to Alaska). He met my mother and they started a family, settling in Holden, his home town. He was trained as a Mechanical Engineer and worked for a company that made bottling machinery. Back in the forties, fifties, and sixties, Worcester was a manufacturing hub. Eventually his company wanted to send him to the Milwaukee area—he would have to relocate and get involved in labor negotiations with unions; if you knew my father, it was not something that would appeal to him. So I think my parents just decided to make a break for it. The two of them were in lock step; they had spent their honeymoon on an island off the Maine coast. And previous to the move, my father had a power boat built by a yard in Maine, so he began to acquire some knowledge of the Maine coast; he was comfortable with navigation, tools, and in a variety of different settings (he had built our house in Massachusetts).

When they decided to make the move, my parents came Downeast and drove around. They crossed the Rockport bridge, looked out at the harbor, thought it looked pretty cool and started inquiring if there were properties available. A family owned lobster business at the head of the harbor, on the shore, had ceased operations; that family decided the future of the lobster business was in Boston; their property was for sale. My parents saw it, liked it, and bought it. In the winter of sixty-one sixty-two my father drove up on weekends to make improvements before we moved; the place was somewhat rundown. He hired help to renovate the main building where we eventually lived, in an apartment above the main floor.

We moved at the end of the school year in June of sixty two, when I was twelve; my sister Sarah is the youngest; she was seven. I thought the move was horrible; things were good in Holden—I had friends. The idea was to open a boatyard, but to get things moving, a source of income was needed. My parents decided to start a restaurant as support until the boatyard was up to speed; Mother went to cooking school. By the time the family moved, the Sail Loft Restaurant was ready to start operations.

I went to the local schools starting in the eighth grade. It took me about two days to realize, once I was in Rockport, that things were pretty good. The restaurant took off, really worked, and both my parents were involved in it. My mother ran the restaurant for lunch during the day, and after a day in the boatyard, my father would act as host in the restaurant at night.

In the early days the boatyard was essentially a service yard. A dock was built; my dad bought a travel lift, built some floats and the customers came. Before I got to high school I was pretty disconnected; I certainly knew what was going on, but it wasn't until high school that I started working part time. I was hanging out with my friends and didn't apply myself at school, although I breezed through pretty easily. At college, when I was away, I began to appreciate how nice it was in Maine. I got into Amherst College (I was probably at the low end of the range) and started thinking I would be a Biology major. But there was too much Math (when Math had more letters than numbers it was a struggle for me); I had a hard time with Calculus, so I ended up a Psychology major which was more to my liking. Bottom line, I had a tough time academically, and I missed the ocean, fresh water fishing, scuba diving, and the friends I had around home.

I came back to Rockport after college and started working for my dad at Rockport Marine. The relationship was good and also difficult; mixing family and business is a tough combination.

As I gained more confidence in my ability, I wanted to do things differently and there were conflicts. At any given moment we had four or five employees. It was still a service oriented yard. I was willing to help and ended up doing a lot of painting, running our work boat to maintain moorings, towing boats around, running people out to their own boats. It was more or less what the dock crew does now.

When I was about thirty I took a course in wooden boat repair methods at the Wooden Boat School in Brooklin, Maine, which was the first year the course was offered. The instructor was Joel White, who I had heard of but never met. We became good friends as a result of the course. He liked my attitude about stuff; I had some ability and knew what I was doing. Prior to that course I had bought an old junker of a boat, a thirty five foot lobster boat, and rebuilt it in my spare time over the course of five years, so I had picked up some woodworking skills. The two week course was fun. He saw in me a person who approached the work in a similar way and offered me a job; that was around 1980. He had received an order to build a fifty foot power boat and asked if I would be interested in joining his group to build the boat. My father was OK with it because he had some sense it was something I really wanted to do. I ended up working for Joe for about a year. Back then the boatyards were much smaller; he had no more than twelve employees, even though he was well known up and down the coast. His son Steve runs the boatyard now, and it is much larger, but it took a while for the wooden boat business to become the size it is today. When I was hired Steve had just returned and we became friends.

Wood is a great material, a great engineering material; it's fun to work with, it's healthy. The people around wooden boats tend to be pretty terrific: people that build them, people that own them. I learned two things building that boat for Joel White: I learned that I really liked the process of building boats. I also learned that I really didn't like to work for other people. It wasn't Joe, not at all. We never stopped being great friends.

I had married in 1973 when I was twenty-four, to a local girl. A child was born just as I was finishing up that year with Joe, in the summer of 1982. My wife stayed in Rockport when I was working in Brooklin, and I would come home on weekends. We divorced in 1986.

I talked to my father in 1982 about coming back to

Rockport and eventually taking over the business. That meant the boatyard, not the restaurant, but I would work into taking over the restaurant later as well, sharing ownership with my sister Lucia (my other brother and sister were not involved in the business at all).

When I came back the focus was on service and repair work, storage of boats during the winter, and re-commissioning them in the spring. That was the bread and butter of the yard; it still is to this day as well. However, we gradually acquired more significant and complicated repair and restoration projects for the winter. I remember a good friend of my father, a hotel guy, bought a power boat which we finished off. In 1988 we took down the building which we had used for our repair and storage space, the building that had been used by the previous owner as the lobster pound. We put up a considerably larger building, built a large dock and purchased a bigger lift—we were then capable of handling more significant projects. My father was still in the business; we butted heads but it worked. In order to buy the business from him, I got to know the bank. I still know the bank. We gradually took on more people, but up until the mid to late nineties it was always a struggle to feel that we had enough work to get us through a winter. If we could get through a winter and still be solvent, it seemed like we had enough to do in the spring, summer, and fall: launching boats, servicing boats, and then hauling boats out in the fall. Winter time was a real crunch time for most boat yards at that time. All the yards were geared up to get enough work to keep a crew on during the winter. For us it was mostly restoration work. It took us a long time to get over that hump.

People who wanted a boat built wanted to know how many boats you had built, to give them confidence that you would finish the project. We didn't have that history, but we finally built a Dark Harbor 20, a 30 foot sailboat popular out on Isleboro. It's a Marconi rig S and S design, a narrow day-sailer; beautiful. We built one speculatively. We didn't make any money on it since we had no reputation, but we sold it, and we kept a crew going. We bought the plans (in this particular case the plans were not expensive). We have built boats on spec at other times and they were sold; it's a form of advertising.

Estates of some designers don't want to let the plans out for any price; they don't want any more boats built. That was the case for Augie Nielsen, a famous designer with a shop in Boston who designed and built some wonderful boats. He stipulated that no other boats were to be built to his designs following his death; he held the builder to a very high standard and wasn't comfortable the boats could continue to be built to that standard without his presence. We spent some time with his estate a few years ago and convinced them that we actually could build to that standard. We got permission from the estate to do so, though we have yet to find a client who wants one built.

The wooden boat yards up and down the coast of Maine work cooperatively with one another. If our customers happen to be in another part of the state, we make sure the yard down there can take care of their needs appropriately; it's terrific! No yard wants to steal your business. If we launch a boat and a problem develops and we get a call, it sometimes works best to have a yard fix the problem locally, where they are. We will set that up and see if the yard can help.

If a project comes our way and I'm not particularly equipped to handle the work, I might suggest they talk to another yard. We've done it for others and others have done it for us.

In 1992 we acquired an off-site property on the Beech Hill Road in Rockport and put up a storage building, because demand for our space exceeded our capacity. We filled that up immediately with a total of ten 40 foot storage boats. A few years after that we put up a second building at the same site. In the mid-nineties a customer with a 40 foot Concordia yawl had us do some work; following that he bought a 45 foot sailboat and had us completely restore it, with major design changes (Joel White did those design changes). We did the restoration work over the course of a winter; the same client kept saying he wanted to build or restore a much larger boat. He eventually spoke to Joel about designing a 76 foot sailboat, which Joel designed. He talked to me about building the boat and he said: "You know, I think I want to build two of them. Why don't you build one and Brooklin Boat Yard can build the other." Neither Joel nor I thought it would ever happen.

There was a wooden boat show in Mystic, Connecticut in 1997; our client stood up and said Rockport Marine and Brooklin Boat Yard were going to build two 76 foot sailboats. He wanted to start a business where he would have these 'one-design' sailboats to sell with the idea of developing a racing circuit up and down the East Coast. So we each built a boat, as well as parts and pieces for each other. Brooklin Boat Yard got started a few months before we could because of various workloads; we ended up helping them get their boat to the client early. When they were finished they turned around and helped us finish off our boat, so we also got our boat to the client early; we launched the boats in 1998. Just prior to that a commission came in for a 32 foot sailboat, and my father had us build a 45 foot power boat which was launched in 1997. Although the racing circuit never happened, we built three 46 foot boats for the original client, two in 1999, and one in 2000-2001. From then on it seemed like we had a new boat to build every year along with our restoration work and our winter storage. We became a little bit larger every year.

In 1988 I had met Joel White's daughter; I knew Joel's whole family before I knew her. She was previously married living in New Hampshire, a writer and editor. I happened to go up to Brooklin to look at a project for Rockport. I stopped in to see Joel and he asked if I wanted to come over for dinner; he didn't know Martha was coming home that night. I was divorced by then, and unbeknownst to me she was divorcing. We met at dinner and had a great time. We started seeing each other after that. She was working for the Farmer's Almanac in Dublin, New Hampshire. She also did freelance work for various publications. We were married in 1991. Her son Sam is now 32 and works for Rockport Marine. I have a son Nathan who is going to be 30 this year; he works in South Korea for the American Bureau of Shipping (ABS), a classification society, in a Hyundai shipyard. He is a surveyor making sure that ships are being built to pre-approved specifications and plans. He graduated from the Maine Maritime Academy. Martha and I also have our own children;

both are in college now.

Regarding overseas shipyards, it is worth noting here that most people who buy luxury yachts today are buying imports. I hope there is enough work for those of us who do quality work here in the US, but to explain, to demonstrate quality, you need to show it. It's not unlike a tailor who displays a suit in the window, and then turns it inside out to show the hand stitching, the lining and finishing. It all comes down to your employees. When a man comes to me for a job I ask a few questions: "Where have you worked before? Let me speak to your previous employer." I observe how he conducts himself (or she conducts herself). I can tell a lot by the kinds of hand tools he has. I supply all the portable power tools, but I expect everyone who is working as a boat builder at Rockport Marine to have their own chisels and planes, hammers and saws. You can tell a lot about someone just by seeing what they have for tools, how they are cared for. Have I ever made a mistake? Absolutely! Of course I have. When I have made a mistake, it just makes the job at hand more difficult. Since we are constantly bidding on projects, even bidding against our friends in Brooklin, we better be right about the capabilities of our own shop, and when that client can buy 30-40% cheaper overseas, our story has to be a good one, an honest one.

We have a new facility in Belfast, Maine, just up the road. For a long time I wanted to have a place where we could haul and work on larger boats. I like doing new things and bigger boats are meatier! I came to the realization that we don't have enough land space in Rockport. We are bumping up against limits of what we can accomplish here; we have to haul some boats up the hill because we can't launch them here. The

215

biggest boat we built here was 115 tons, around 85 feet on deck.

I looked around and talked to some other yards; then Steve White was looking too. The site in Belfast is a former sardine packing plant; that plant had been idle for at least ten years. I was aware of the site and knew it would be a beautiful site for a boatyard, with four or five acres of flat land, which is a real rarity, right on deep water. Two developers had already been there, but then we got word that the latest developer was going bankrupt; the site might be available. Steve and I and a guy named J.B. Turner got together and ultimately acquired the property. J.B. became our new Managing Director. He had previously worked for a long time at Lyman Morse in Thomaston, Maine. Prior to that he was Manager of Wayfarer Marine in Camden, Maine, and before that managed a boatyard in Connecticut where he grew up. Like Steve and me, he had been in the boat business his whole life and developed a great reputation. The three of us often went to boat shows together; we were like a loose organization, to help defray costs. We have similar philosophies of how to operate a boatyard. We bought what became the boatyard in Belfast, from the previous owners, out of state developers who had wanted to build condominiums, but were bankrupt. There are actually six partners in the business: three of us, my sister Lucia, Ken Priest (he runs a company in Augusta called the Kenway Corporation), and Jack Rennick from Florida.

It was really an abandoned site, and the city of Belfast was in court with the previous owners over contractual issues they had failed to live up to. We were required to tear down an

216

existing building on the site; then we cleaned up the site, built a dock, bought a travel lift and started putting up buildings. Lo and behold, fast forward, we are quite busy in Belfast. But it was really something out of nothing. We closed on the property in mid-January 2011 and opened the business seven months after that. Word got out pretty quick that we were developing a yard. J.B., the Managing Director, is the reason I'm involved—he is such a good guy with a great following: people that work for him and customers. He is the perfect one to run the yard; none of the rest of us interfere. We are there to help him, when he needs it, but it's really his yard to run. It's because of him that all the business has come in.

J.B.'s history has been more with the composite end of the business. He is much more experienced than the rest of us with fiberglass and the higher tech carbon composites as well as aluminum. Boats of that type are the thrust of the business being developed. It's storage through the winter, repair and restoration, and, we hope, new boat construction. It's a fully functioning boatyard independent of Brooklin Boat Yard and Rockport Marine. It's another competitor.

A man brought a 106 foot aluminum motor yacht from New Jersey last fall. The structural elements of the boat, the hull and deck, are aluminum; the interior is nicely finished in wood and there are teak decks. Belfast is doing a complete re-fit of the boat, a complete restoration of a boat 25 years old that hasn't been used much by the owner in the last 5 years. The captain of the boat had a previous relation with J.B.

We actually hauled one of our boats in Belfast we couldn't haul here and did some work on it. Our mobile hoist has a 55 ton capacity (maybe a 70 foot boat) but the lift in Belfast has a

155 ton capacity (130-140 foot boat). If I was to acquire a large building or restoration project I couldn't accomplish here, we'd figure out a way to do it in Belfast. I don't know if that means my crew would do it or J.B.'s crew or we'd do it jointly. I know it's unheard of, but it really works well; we trust each other implicitly. It's really a trust business for the six of us.

The last boat we built at Rockport Marine was in 2007-2008. Ever since then the work has been restoration, complete restorations to the point they are virtually a new boat. We've done five multi-year projects in the past five years. In 2008 when things really tanked (I was actually working on my own boat), one of our customers had to cut the pace of his project in half; a dozen of my people were working on his boat. All of a sudden we had to go down to six; I had to let a few people go, which I hate doing. That was my signal to start trying to acquire projects: pay attention to scuttlebutt, visit people. We go to boat shows, but it never seems to bring in business (there are other good reasons for going). I have never acquired a project as a direct result of a boat show or advertisement. Most of our business comes by word of mouth, from satisfied customers.

Several years ago I bought an old 76 foot sardine carrier, and we're in the middle of restoring it although we haven't worked on it recently. If we get really slow, I'll get started on that again. We built a house on a bluff adjoining the yard mostly for the same reason. If the yard gets slow, I can keep a cohesive crew by putting them on another project. It's the key to operating a successful yard that does the kind of work we do. The people who work on the boats are the key to the success of this business. I can't afford to lose a core group of really competent people. Right now there are probably fifty-five of us; I'm sixty-three. Nothing changes; up and down the coast we're all looking for projects.

Luis Lopez

Movie actor handsome, determined, always there to help, a family man

When I came to this country, I wanted to learn something; I bought books and kept on practicing and practicing with computers. I took them apart and put them back together again. You have to walk away, go to bed sometimes. I figure if it doesn't work this way probably another way; then I get up. I go to Google; Google gives me a lot of information and I start using that information. You go to Google and you plug in a question. That's what I do and Google will answer you and you'll see how many people are having the same problem and you're not alone. Someone there is telling you what to do and you see: click right here and all of a sudden something appears that says correct your computer for free but you find so many mistakes so you say fix it and it says you have to register and buy the software. They keep on getting you.

I have everything on the shelf in here: The Power of Positive Thinking, Creating Compositions, English for Meaning, The Minority Career Book. Dynamite Answers to Interview Questions: I bought that one at the University Store. Someone took that book, the complete edition that had all the quotes in Spanish and English—that was fantastic; I loved that book. That's how I knew that here in America they don't use quotations; we use a lot of quotations in Colombia. If you use those quotations you can simplify long conversations, like using An error doesn't become a mistake until you refuse to correct it, something like that when you say those words; from where I come from we use a lot of those quotations and it's beautiful.

I'm from Popayán; there's a lot of writers from there, famous writers and poets, the southern part of Colombia; it is in between hot and cold although I understand like in the United States, the climate is changing. When I was a kid I remember, I was eight years old and we moved to another city, but I remember before we moved it was kind of chilly in the morning, a little bit warmer in the afternoon, comfortable, and at six o'clock it started getting cooler again, the entire year in Popayán, I think because it's near the equator; that's very possible. Nowadays in Popayán it's not as cold as it was before; now the temperature I would say is in the 30s centigrade; it's warmer.

We moved to Cali up north from Popayán—that's a tropical place; you see a lot of Palms, like in California or Las Vegas. My parents wanted to move up there; I have no reason—I don't know; I was so small I didn't ask questions, but he was a professor at the School of Arts. He used to teach how to design shoes for women and men, and he had his own business making shoes. He had people all over the city working for him; the name of the business was Royal Shoes— handmade shoes; he had people making shoes at home; he had quite a few guys working at the store, in the back of the store—you wouldn't get to see them, all you would see was a shoe display. If you wanted my father to design your shoe he would go from scratch.

I lived in Cali from the age of eight until I moved to the United States; I went to school there. When we moved from Popayán to Cali I had already finished my elementary school.

221

As a matter of fact I started at a little school and from there I went on to Melvin Jones, a good school where they taught a little English.

When we moved to Cali I went to Santa Librada, a very good public school. My brothers went to Catholic school, private school just around the block from where we lived, so they got better opportunities. I would say being the oldest you lose a lot of good opportunities; you're always the black sheep; that way you're the one who gets the worst part of it and I think that happens in every family. I think it's a matter of culture too, but it wasn't easy for me in my early years; they were miserable; I was miserable. Both my father and my mother had no compassion, no compassion whatsoever. They used to beat me, both my father and my mother. My mother is still living and I take care of her; she says she doesn't remember any of that; if I tell her she doesn't want to hear. I was a very active and energetic kid; probably that was part of it.

I remember one day I was with my brother (he was two years younger), and we stopped at my father's store. My father told me he says we needed to run an errand. We got to the National Building, there were these steps and on the side of the steps like a bannister beside the steps you can slide on, so I did, and guess what, I lost my grip. I hit the pavement with my head, first time like in the comics when they see little stars; I saw them, physically. So anyway we continued my brother and I down the block. We did what we were supposed to do, then we came back to my father's store. We didn't say anything to my father about what happened to me but I was kind of worried. My father said: I want you to go to Rodolfo Zuñiga (he was the owner of another big shoe store). I want you to bring this to him; I said okay Dad. We're talking about 1-2-3-4-5 blocks from one to the other and my brother was still with me when I got to the other store. I said to the owner, Do you see something in my eyes, do you see something in my eyes now? No, he said, they look normal to me. I said to him I don't know I just hit my head and I cannot see too good. Something bothers me right now. We left, from there to the Basilica, only one block accross the park. When I got there I started crying and I said to my brother: Ovidio, Ovidio, please give me your hand. He said, what is it? I said: I cannot see, I'm blind. I lost my sight. Take me inside the Cathedral; I want to pray. So he took me inside. I start praying and I was crying and I was very loud because can you imagine from one moment to the next becoming blind, losing your eyesight? For me it was a terrible experience! So we got out of there together (I still couldn't see) back to my father's store and we told my father about the conditions, but unfortunately now ignorance always pays a price. My father was going to hit me instead of taking me to the doctor. A good thing that one of the people who worked for my father, my aunt, says: you're not going to touch him in that condition—you're not going to beat him up no way, so he took me to a pharmacist and he gave me something. As a matter of fact I had blurry vision all of a sudden; I was walking behind someone and I thought it was my father. My Dad grabbed me and pulled me back and I said oh I thought that was you Dad. He took me home and I lay down. The pharmacist said take 10 drops in water. I fell asleep and when I woke up nobody was at home; my brother who was supposed to be with me was outside; he was playing soccer so I started screaming and he came in. I said: Ovidio please, can you give me that medication? I started with a dropper even with my tears; one, two, three.... Then my mother came—she was at church and she brought a doctor. The doctor said: can you see? I said no. Later my mother told me he grabbed a teaspoon and put a candle in front of the teaspoon and he held it up and said, can you see that? I said I can see a little light. He left; I was like that for three days. I lost my eyesight and they all knew that I had fallen; there was no need to hide it anymore. Years later while I was going to school in Cali, and my brother was going to the same school, we were in one of those recesses and crossing the soccer field together and somebody kicked the ball and it hit me right here on the side of my head, and I was already blind again. They took me to the school infirmary—I don't know what they gave me, but it relaxed me and a few minutes later I began seeing again. Another occasion in Cali we're laying in bed six o'clock in the afternoon my mother and my brother and my sister we were in bed talking. All of a sudden a violent tremor; everybody ran outside and somehow I hit my head in the rush and I fell asleep; when I woke up a good thing that I could see but I wanted to say water but I said something different. Why is it that I cannot make the connection? Why is it I am saying shoe?

I decided to go to school at night time and find a job which I did and I must have been at this time probably 17. I did not receive a diploma at the high school. No, I did not receive a secondary certificate in Colombia. I started working the same time I was going to school; that was a normal thing to do so I started working for Banco del Comercio. I used to be on a bicycle going around the city delivering statements (I believe it was) to the customers and then I would go to night school but to be quite honest with you I wasn't paying much attention at school. It was boring and I was tired. From there while I was still going to school I got another job with the Banco Cafetero that was a little better job. I kept moving up at that bank and then I applied to Banco Bogotá. They moved me around to different branches but they found out that my sister was working for the same entity so they told me either my sister or I would have to give up the job; those were the rules. So I applied for a company Almaviva de Colombia. They did more with imports than exports and they had another business under the same name that used to sell steel rods for construction. I was asked to do an audit and found out that Alfonso my friend was stealing money. I didn't say anything to him but I went directly to the big guy and they investigated and Alfonso unfortunately ended up in jail. After that they sent me to the Port of Buenaventura on the Pacific Ocean—that was a promotion, and I lived there for about a year. The Port was nice; and when I wanted to have access to the ships at the pier, my boss Andres Clarkson let me used his pass—he was the chief of the office (Imports) over there and I made a lot of money there.

I didn't come to the United States to put my hands on dollars because I had plenty of dollars, probably money I never had in the U.S. There I had my ways—I had my clients; they used to call me from Cali and say can you deliver? So I said let me see; I'll work on the Manifest. So I could fast track their deliveries and they would compensate me. I intervened with Customs and since I had access to the pier (Andres gave me his ID), I could buy a lot of stuff from different countries and I used to hide that stuff because when you got out of the Port the police always had a checkpoint and they had quite a few all along the road. I used to hide them so good—it wasn't legal because it never passed Customs. I brought this stuff to my Mom and I said to my Mom don't worry; keep the money. I did really well, incredible, and yet nowadays when I remind my Mom I used to bring these things she forgot but yet she didn't forget. I was there and I had it very good; they treated me good—the native people treated me good; the black people they were nice. I was around 18 when I eventually came back to Cali and I applied for Fruco of Colombia. They used to make canned soup and all that stuff. I remember as an employee I could buy fresh chickens, a lot of stuff, a lot of product that they used for their production. I brought all that stuff into my house to my mother, to feed the family. We weren't poor but I helped that way. Besides, one thing which is very important—all the time that I worked my mother imposed a monthly quota; she used to take more than half of my paycheck. As a matter of fact, ever since I can remember even when we were living in Popayán, I never had the happiness of having one summer for myself because they always put me to work. Finish elementary school? They put me to work in carpentry, sweeping, doing something, making a couple of pesos. I didn't get to see that money; that money was for my mom. It really made a very miserable kid. I have worked all my life, nonstop.

Anyway, going back to Cali, working for Fruco, I applied to work for the best bank Banco De La Republica, and I remember my father's brother in law had a very good position there. I can help you he said as long as you pass that test because there's a test here and it's very difficult. I said I don't care; I think I'm ready to take the test. So they gave me a test and I passed. I was given a good position—they treated me so good, incredible. It's so nice when people treat you in a very special way. I was sitting in the back room and I used to have my secretary. She was the daughter of one of the ministers of the government of Colombia. She wasn't a pretty girl but she was very very nice; she was in love with me and I reciprocated in certain ways. She had a very big nose—I think she was a Jewish descendent. Her father was a health minister or something like that. I was at her house a couple times.

That was when I decided to come to the United States, because I was tired of living a disorganized life, a lot of partying. It got to the point where my mother didn't see me on the weekends at all. On the weekends I used to get together with my cousins, go to the family farm, take a bunch of girls out there. A life like that is not giving you anything. We used to have a wonderful time, but again, don't forget, I needed money because it was the policy of the bank that you had to wear a tie every single day—you had to be very presentable. I didn't have enough money left to support myself; remember my mother was taking more than half my paycheck. This idea of leaving; it was really getting away from my mother, getting away from both of them. I never had much communication with my father and one day, we were sitting at a tiny table eating. I remember my father's mother, my grandmother, was there. She was blind (at that time there was no cure for glaucoma). I said to my father let's be friends let's be more communicative between you and I. Who me, he said? Pow! He hit me so hard—I remember I was eating a bowl of soup; blood started dripping into my soup. It didn't matter how virtuous I was, how many things I tried to do for them; I wasn't the bad guy I told them that they thought I was. Nothing seemed to work, so I got to the point where I gave up. I said okay fine, so I started saving my money. I paid a guy to do all my papers; he even purchased my ticket and everything. But before I did that I said to my Mom: listen, I decided to go to the United States, look for different opportunities although I have very good opportunities over here; I'm kind of fed up. I want to be on my own; I want your permission to keep my money at least for three months. In three months I will be gone but I need this money—I need to save a little bit of money to bring with me and at the same time to pay the individual who is doing all my papers, so I need your help. I've been helping you all my life and just now I am only asking you to help me for three months. She said let me talk to your father and later she came back to me and she said: look, for the next three months you can sleep here, but we're not going to feed you anymore, neither clean your clothes, your dirty laundry. But, I said, what kind of help is that Mom? Well, either take it or leave it, she said. I had no choice, so I said fine. Then somebody told me about this lady she used to have a corner store, very nice lady, so I spoke to her. I work for the bank and I also work with someone you know (someone she knew in the neighborhood), so if you want a reference you can talk to that person. She said no, no problem. I can take care of your dirty laundry and I can feed you here for very little money. I said thank you so much it's just going to be for three months. So she did and I slept at home. I kept my money but I was resentful of my father all those years and although I didn't go back to Colombia from the U.S. for 10 years, when I went back my father even then was not very friendly with me and my mother the same. So that made me remember, even 10 years later how I used to come home from working at the bank, how they used to beat me. You know, for lunch they send you home from the bank and you can sleep for a few hours. They beat me so badly they cut my skin and then I had to change my white shirt so I could go back to work.

When I went back to Colombia my father was working for the Air Force. I said: do you guys want to live in the United States? I'll put in for you guys, my brothers and my sisters....everybody. They thought about it and said they thought it was a good idea, so when I came back here I started all the procedures. In fact I became so good at it I was able to help other people. In the end I got everybody here: father mother, my two brothers, my sister. A couple years later I brought my other sister and her husband and all her kids and on another occasion I brought my mother's cousin and his wife and all their kids all for free. The only thing I charged them for was when I had to go to Washington and go before three judges; and don't forget, all the papers had to be translated into English which I did. My brothers started going to college here; one became an architect, the other became a biomedical engineer. They did wonders. God bless them.

One day years later I said to my father I have something

that just won't let me live until I get an answer; I want you to be honest with me. Why, when I was coming to the United States you didn't forgive me for not paying for the last 3 months. My father said: I swear to God I never said that to your Mom; I never did that to you; that was a decision totally of your mother. My father became an asthmatic person—I used to take him to the hospital, rushed him to the emergency room sometimes twice in one night. Go to work the following day. When they first came to the U.S they had some money they brought from Cali. I bought them a house—the house was not in a move-in condition but I said this has a lot of potential and I can help you since I used to work second shift at General Motors at that time. I came out at 12 midnight every night and go directly to that house on the way to my house and stopped right there; I worked there until three or four o'clock in the morning (they were staying with my brother at the time). I did that every single night until the house looked absolutely beautiful. I'm not saying I did everything myself but I sacrificed myself after my working hours. They were very happy there and I helped them even after that, every day. My father purchased this shoe repair shop on Broad Street in Trenton, so he said how am I going to manage this? I told him, well, when I'm on layoff I can help you. You don't have to pay me anything of course but I will help you. I just want you to keep on working. He started repairing shoes at that time and he says what will we call the place? And of course we called it Royal Shoe Repair. It was right across from the YMCA—he stayed there for about a year or so; he did pretty good not bad. He was making enough money to support his wife—it was excellent. Then he closed the place and went to work for a company in Trenton; he was in his early 60s. He became a leather cutter for this company. He did pretty good there until the company started declining because of the economy. A lot of people got laid off so he retired; anyway he had these asthma attacks so it was really time. His pension was practically nothing, however, and my mother used to make his life miserable. I remember my father received a check from Social Security because my sister was still under age; my mother wanted my father to give her that money. I said to her all my father has is $500 a month, miserable $500; she was looking for money money money and she saved money all the time. The first 10 years I was here, when I was supporting my wife and three children, I used to send my mother a money order every week, and when I remind her about the money, she says what money. It really hurts me—that's her way to really get you, and as a matter of fact, she just bought a nice apartment in Florida, in Sunrise, Florida. It's possible my brother bought the apartment for her.

In all the years that I've been here, the first few years I suffered a lot. The first year I used to cry so much, but I said no way am I going back there. I always had a return ticket but even though I had a return ticket I wasn't going back. I refused to go back.

My first wife was from Puerto Rico; I met her when I got here. One night I had the opportunity to meet these people so they took me out and I met a young beautiful girl who used to be an actress and we all went to a party. We got to the party and this little woman with a beautiful face (not the actress) she kind of put her eyes on me. She was a very good dancer—I consider myself a very good dancer. We started dancing and dancing; I didn't pay any more attention to the actress who eventually got drunk and vomited like no end—poor thing. This one was like a little devil and later on she became my wife because she was pregnant; it was a moral obligation. Those friends even bought my wedding ring; they did everything for me. They were the Burgos family from Trenton; they were involved a little in politics. They knew the Commissioner, the State Treasurer, and he was the one who gave me a letter. This girl who became my wife took it to General Motors; she spoke for me at General Motors and she showed them the letter. That got me a good job. My first job was with a printing company in Trenton, printing on plastic. I never worked in a factory before; I came from an office where I was Señor López at the bank. Over here I was just a number; it was a sweatshop. I had so many accidents—all the time I was in the emergency room because I burned my hand, because one of the rolls fell on my foot. I was making $.90 an hour; it was 1963. I didn't know whether it was good or bad money. I was here for a purpose; I wanted to become someone. Then, about a year later, I was laid off from the printing company—I remember I was crying again. I spoke to John Patricio who was a supervisor at the printing company. I said to him what am I going to do? I'm all alone in this country. He said you can take care of the toilets. It was an old building and the toilets really smelled bad.

I couldn't believe it when I got the job at General Motors and they started me at $4.75 an hour. I also had a lot of odd jobs during those years in addition to General Motors because

you have to remember in ten years maybe I had two solid
years at General Motors. There were a lot of layoffs, so in the
meantime I said I'm not wasting my time; I came over here to
make money somehow. There was this neighbor, his name
was Ken Olson. He had his own business replacing driveways.
He said to me: well, you look pretty strong to me—you want
to work with me? He said be ready tomorrow at seven o'clock.
I remember we went up to this driveway and he gave me a
sledgehammer. Okay, I want you to break up the entire
driveway with the sledgehammer and I did it (I used to lift
weights). The following day we put down blacktop. A
neighbor when we moved worked for a beer distributor so I
went with him. I used to go down in the basement; he drove
the truck—we threw cases to each other. I worked with a
group of Costa Ricans doing roofing and I also fitted
insulation. I got up at four o'clock in the morning; we used to
go as far away as Englishtown. It was a very very tough life.

There was this beautiful Irish girl who lived above us,
upstairs. She looked like an angel, long blond hair, beautiful.
One day I was outside in the morning warming up my car
sitting right there and when I looked upstairs she was there in
the window in a nightgown —she blew me a kiss. So I blew a
kiss back—these kinds of things continued in the wintertime.
Still no physical contact. In the summer time it was one of
those occasions when I was laid off again. I was working at
that time for Coleman Oldsmobile on Olden Avenue; I told
them I knew how to paint cars—they gave me an opportunity
to work at the body shop. I said I had worked in my father's
body shop in Colombia which of course was a white lie. I said
give me 30 days and I'll prove it to you and in less than 30

days I proved that I could do it. The first car that I painted was my supervisor's at General Motors. One day I'm in the body shop and I look over the fence and there was that beautiful Irish girl. She called me over—I came over here because your wife doesn't feel good. I went downstairs and she is having one of those crises (actually my wife used to have emotional problems). She needs you to come home; please, go with me. So I went home with her—we came to my house and don't forget, she was my neighbor; she lived upstairs. When we got home I discovered that my wife had taken a sleeping pill and she was asleep. In the meantime we sat in the living room and the girl says to me: you have such beautiful eyes. I like you I like you a lot. Now I knew that her husband had been very abusive—he used to beat her up; she was actually a singer in her husband's musical band. Suddenly we kissed each other.

A few days later she said you know your wife has been unfaithful to you. I said I do not believe that. Why don't you believe me, she asked? I said because you already showed interest in me. You'll do anything to finish my marriage. I tell you what, she said. Next week you're going to a party—your wife invited me. The guy who is your wife's lover is going to be at the party. Well, we're all there at the party; she says, in a few minutes your wife will go behind the stage to meet him because he's over there waiting. Sure enough that happened, even though I didn't get to see the guy. Still I was doubtful whether this was really the case. One night my wife decided to go somewhere; she was going to help a friend with a permanent. She said: drive me over and pick me up later—I'll give you a call and you can pick me up. I take her over and when I got back to the apartment I heard someone crying, so I went to the back. I opened the window because the Irish lady's entrance was on that side of the house. I called to her. What are you doing? She said: so many things I wish for. I said okay, I'll open the back door; you want to come over? So she came down and within seconds we were so tightly engaged in such a passionate moment you cannot possibly imagine. We broke the bed. This is not something you prepare for—it just happened spur of the moment. Anyway, I had already suspicions that my wife was being unfaithful to me. I was working third shift for this company across the river, so one night I decided to go have lunch from over there to my home; I was doing that for a reason—it was in the middle of the night, one o'clock, something like that. There she was, just took a shower, nothing on under her robe. I was convinced she was waiting for someone. A few days later I definitely confirmed the fact and the lady upstairs confirmed that he'd been to the house quite a few times.

I continued my relationship with this lady for quite a few years. Her husband was out there playing with his band every weekend. She treated me like a king—what a wonderful woman, what a beautiful woman! She learned to speak Spanish; she played Spanish music when I used to walk into her house. It was like walking into a palace—she looked so beautiful, so wonderful. But she got obsessed, and I don't like women like that. When I went back to work at General Motors I pulled out of the parking lot and she would be there in her car, with everybody coming out of General Motors. Thank goodness nobody knew that she was there for me but it was still very embarrassing. She said one day, let's take off; if you don't want my son I'll give him to my mom—this really turned me off. Her son besides everything else had a hearing problem and that's that.

I took a trip to Colombia and I went to the city to one of those witch doctors, whatever they're called, and I said to him I want to get rid of this person. He said yes; you know, when you came over here she became very sick but she met someone and that person has been taking care of her (she was not living with her husband anymore at that point). I want to finish this I said to him. He said, I want you to do this, and this and this. You'll see that everything will work itself out. I bought a beautiful gold chain for her. When I got back I called her and I said hi, how are you doing? I got a little something for you. She says yes, I would like to see you—I have something to tell you. So we got together; she said you know one day when I was at work I lost consciousness. I was very sick and you didn't tell me you were going to Colombia or how long you are going to be out of town, and I became very sick and during my stay in the hospital one of my fellow workers started taking care of me every single day and I've kind of fallen for him. I gave her the present and that was the end of it.

Of course I was supporting my wife and three children all this time. From the time she deserted me I had to pay child support for many many years. As a matter of fact when I met my present wife Martha, I told her of the situation and when we got married she agreed. She said don't worry about it; I will help you with that situation. Three years later I discovered, I found out that my older daughter had been married two years before, so I went to the office of child support and I told them about the situation and they gave me credit. All these little things actually happened to me.

I was in the process of getting my divorce when I met Martha; I think I met Martha pretty soon after. She was very young, 16 the first time I knocked on her parents' apartment door—I wanted to visit her uncle. I fell instantly in love with her; I remember that day I got there at 11 o'clock and I walked out of there about 11 o'clock that night. I spoke to her mother—I explained to both of them my situation, I didn't hide anything, nothing at all. I wanted to put everything right on the table because there was interest in both of us so the best thing was just to be honest. Her mother allowed me to visit her even though I was still in the process of getting a divorce and besides I had three children, and frankly it was not that I was looking to enter a relationship, and then she was still in high school, Princeton High School! I said to her mother one day I would like to take her out to dinner so her mother said okay you can take her out to dinner but the latest you can bring her home is 10:30 or 11 o'clock. I said no problem she will be here at that time. Martha said, you know when I first met you I wanted to know what kind of car you were driving (that's woman's curiosity—they always want to see a guy driving a nice luxury car). She had gone upstairs and looked out the window when I first left the house, and she thought I had a real old car, but you know, she said she didn't care. That Saturday, when I went to pick her up for dinner, I opened up the door of my car and she saw that I had a beautiful car; no one had a car like that in this area, with swivel seats; that car it looked like a mafioso car—it had a tire on the trunk. It was quite a car. I had sound equipment in there -it was absolutely incredible.

That was probably in the year 1974 and I was working at General Motors at the time (I was 28 years at General Motors; after the first ten years it got pretty steady, not that much with layoffs). So after about three months she decided to come over to my house. I said I don't want you to be here; this is my house. Then things got really complicated because my ex-wife decided to come back to my house; she came back to live there. She claimed she was still my wife and it's her house, so how can I throw her out of the house? At that point Martha said I will step aside. I said I'd really appreciate that. In the meantime we'll see what happens. So about a month later my unstable wife went into a violent fit which she had done previously. She cut my arm with a knife, she ripped my clothes, she ripped her clothes, then she went upstairs. All of a sudden the police came to the house; they said your wife just called the police. You're beating her up. I haven't touched her; she is the one—she cut me. Look I'm bleeding. I haven't touched her; I'm not the type of person who would touch a woman or abuse a woman. She came downstairs (she had put on makeup with a black eye). The police said to me we're asking you to leave the house. But, I said, I haven't done anything (the three kids were right there!). Otherwise we're going to have to arrest you. I don't know why, but she packed up and left with the kids! As soon as she left I ran to the store and I changed the locks. It was the weekend—I went to New York to party. The hell with this, I said. I don't have this one and the other one, the other one is in recession. Let me go to

New York; I'll have a great time in New York—I stayed the weekend in New York. When I got back the house was totally empty. She had cleaned out the whole house. Years later when we started talking to each other again I asked her what happened that night; you didn't have the house key anymore. Oh, I called the police and I said you know I live right here and I lost my key. Could you be so kind as to let me into my house, and the policeman was such a gentleman he let her into the house. The kids later said you know we love you so much and our mother really took advantage of you. She remarried ever since.

A little time after that I made up with Martha. I used to sleep on the floor on a little mattress right there. So the divorce was finally settled and Martha said to me, you know I want to be with you all the time, and I said, you know honey I'm not ready for that—I'm just not ready for that and she said, yes but you're all by yourself here. There she is sitting on the steps of my house. I said to her you're crazy! She's only 18 at that point; of course she's free of her parents, not under the care of her parents. She's an adult now. I told her maybe you better think it over; I'm much older than you are; you're a beautiful girl, like an angel to me. I'm not ready to enter another relationship right now. Maybe right now it really doesn't make much difference. She started crying and crying. I don't care what you say; I love you; I want to do this—this is what I want to do. So I said, well we can give it a try. To this day she still throws that in my face: you never asked me to marry you. I say to her, you never walked that path that I had to walk in my life.

Things happened very, very nicely. We agreed a few

weeks later, and she moved in, still not married. We lived together for about three years (no babies) until we got married. Then we were ready, and meantime I found her a job at General Motors. We got married and started a family—it's been wonderful. I was 36 when we got married and she was 20. I had been going to college, but when I was going through my divorce I had so much stress I stopped going to classes. Martha said, I always said I wanted to have a professional as a husband. If you are not going to be a professional you are not going to be my husband. I said what my problem is I don't have the money to finish, which was not actually the case, but that's what I told her. I don't have the money to finish. If I get through this semester, and I pass, then I'll get reimbursed by General Motors. One day she showed up with the money and said, no more excuses about going back to school. So I had no other way but to go back to college.

You should see all the beautiful rings I have, all those rings that she gave me. Even when she was a student in high school she went to that shop in Princeton, that jewelry shop in Princeton on Nassau Street. And she bought me a ring. She has given me so much, so much. I love her dearly, we recently celebrated our 34 years wedding anniversary in Las Vegas.

APPENDIX

Alfred Wolf – Flight Log

June 1929

It was a lovely spring evening in 1929. Prohibition reigned, which meant that by the time the clear sky was lit only by the stars and moon, both of us were feeling no pain. The lovely young lady and her 24 year old companion were seated on the flat, suburban Philadelphia lawn reclining against a convenient 45 degree bank observing the heavens. An immense sausage-like object slid across our field of vision, passing silently, slowly, almost majestically from below our feet to beyond our heads. It was the Graf Zeppelin on a visit to our country.

Countless tales have been told by sundry airmen ascribing such incidents and others as the inspiration that triggered their desire to fly. I have tried to attribute my flying to many experiences which I learned of by ear or the written word. Seeing Halley's Comet was a popular one. But when Mother held me up to the window to see, I felt no urge to reach out or follow it. My first sight of an aircraft in flight when I was approaching my 7th birthday at Ventnor, New Jersey, only made me aware of the curious grinding noise the two-propeller Wright biplane made, more like a giant cricket than any other mechanically generated noise. I didn't rush to my parents and ask for a real or even a toy airplane for my birthday.

When my parents took the four of us on our grand tour of the United States in 1919, we saw the mail-carrying Jennies at Chicago Airport; they merited a shot with my Brownie

241

camera, but certainly they neither tempted me to inspect or ride in them, nor planted in me any thought of flight.

I had a fearless brother four years older, and when our tour took us to Santa Barbara a few weeks later, we wandered along the northern shore and came upon a Curtiss Flying Boat with four holes for humans in its whale-like fuselage; the crew of two sought customers to fly with then at five dollars apiece. My brother had three dollars and asked me to lend him two dollars. Feeling like a judge who had just handed down a death sentence I loaned him the money. He survived, but we both kept the event secret from our parents.

Then came the night Lindbergh was aloft over the ocean and the day following. My brother clung to the makeshift radio we owned which, sunspots (etc.) permitting, one could hear KDKA in Pittsburgh detailing the event; I thought he was crazy. The net result? I failed to unearth anything like the romantic moments others had described, in books, or from the dais, or in conversation, that inspired them to fly.

My first flight came about in a terribly reasonable way. Possibly I received encouragement from the wonderful sight and mellow mood I enjoyed with the young lady that June evening. Not many days later I was seated at my office desk with nearly two years of law practice under my belt when a fellow member of the Bar called to suggest that on June 16th I should play hooky and join him with a couple of other friends to see the Graf Zeppelin in Lakehurst, New Jersey. He had chartered a plane (and pilot) from Pitcairn Aviation at Horsham, Pennsylvania, and there was not only room for me, but the price was such that he needed a full house. He had offered a better excuse than golf or something similar for not working; close inspection of the giant floating sausage had to be interesting – I joined up.

Pitcairn Field in Willow Grove, Pennsylvania (later a Naval Air Station) was a meadow lying along a much travelled turnpike about an hour from City Hall, Philadelphia. Its opening had marked the first giant step heralding the growth of Harold Pitcairn's amazing career in aviation, when he moved the core of his sundry activities from Bryn Athyn, Pennsylvania, where he had his first factory and airfield (at what later became the site of the Academy of the New Church). In 1929, at Pitcairn Field, one saw four types of aircraft Harold manufactured: the Orowing, the Fleetwing, the Mailwing, and the "Hopship" (a bastard). One also saw successive prototype autogyros (the rotating wing predecessors of the helicopter), aircraft of other manufacturers, and customers' stored and parked aircraft.

On our arrival at Pitcairn, when we had made ourselves known, we were introduced to Jim Faulkner, our pilot. Jim led us to a Wright whirlwind-powered, high-wing monoplane: a Curtiss Robin. It was this aircraft that flew us to and from Lakehurst. I was surprised to discover that I was neither scared nor did I have a tendency toward airsickness. We seemed to hit few of what the laity then termed "air pockets," and bumps were certainly minor compared to that era's vintage cars on the average road. The weather was fine, and on the whole I enjoyed the hour and a half of my first flight.

What annoyed me, and has since proven to be a most cogent reaction to a first VFR flight, was my inability to recognize where we were. Jim Faulkner had provided me with three maps (in those days we used the back side of the Rand

McNally state maps, overprinted in red with airport sites), and I was given Pennsylvania and New Jersey maps marked with our route. But just after takeoff (and on descent) I got disoriented, and never before having had a first rate sense of direction, I was dismayed. By the time we landed back at Pitcairn, however, I had begun to entertain a belief, strengthened with the years, that flying could be useful. Had a business reason taken me to Lakehurst that afternoon, what an easy way to go. Was I to live near an airport and commute to work or play, I could free myself from the innumerable, unhappy consequences of surface travel!

After landing I took Jim aside and asked him how I might learn how to fly. Jim pointed to an Orowing parked nearby and said, "Climb in there, I'll show you." I explained that I was totally inept mechanically--I could not drive a nail successfully, and if anyone took a pair of scissors apart, I was not sure I could reassemble it. Jim's answer was, "Do you want to learn to fly it or repair it? And are you going to climb out and put it together while it's flying?" Jim had won. We went over to the Orowing and checked the gas and oil; he lent me a helmet and goggles hanging from the stick in the rear cockpit. I climbed in and fastened my seatbelt.

There was little to explain; Jim showed me the throttle, rudders and stick. He told me the rudders worked opposite to the controls on a Flexible Flyer sled, that whenever I pushed the stick, the plane would sink, and vice versa. He showed me a tachometer, an oil temperature gauge and a magnetic compass. His only real concern, it seemed, was the function of the switch. As he had to crank the OX5 Engine by hand, he made me repeat his instructions respecting the signals "contact" and "off". What he called the "Lunky" for short (the

Lunkenhamer), was what was later called the "Primer." I got full instructions on its use.

Jim hoped the engine would start immediately, which OX5's usually did in the warm weather. Before cranking the prop by hand Jim explained he would start flying, and when up, lacking a Gosport tube, he would turn the plane over to me by putting both hands in the air (he would be seated in the front cockpit). I was to keep the nose on the horizon and the wings level. He did not bother to explain runs to me on this baptismal flight. He jumped in and off we went.

I still have my first log book (sold to me at Pitcairn that day). It reads as follows:

Date	No. of Flight	Time in Air	Plane	Nature of Flight
6/16/29	1	0.05	Orowing	Instruction

Needless to say, Jim was too wise to keep me up too long and by chance scare me away. I was not thrilled, nor was I scared. But I was challenged and definitely hooked. On nine more evenings that month, Log Book #1 tells me I flew a half hour each day but one, and that one day I got in 40 whole minutes! Because most students arrived after work, or because, as the instructors said, students learned more readily during a lesson of 30 minutes, I rarely got in more than 30 minutes until I soloed, and we never had Gosport tubes or other communication devices other than hand signals.

It may be interesting at this point to explain a Gosport tube to readers brought up in the second half of the 20th century. I was raised in a three story home where Mother was in the kitchen, pantry or cellar, or on the 3rd floor; we called through hollow

245

tubes built into the walls and through the floors. These tubes were more advanced than the Gosport tubes found on more advanced airplanes, for each had a whistling lid at its outlet operated by a hearty breath. One spoke through the tube unassisted by wires or amplification. I found myself envious of a fellow student, Bill Page, who had bought a U.S. Gypsy Moth (an airplane built in Haverhill, Massachusetts) which had a Gosport. Even though Bill's tube lacked a whistle, it never failed, as the earpieces were fastened to your head by sockets in your helmet; thus you were always in touch in both directions.

There were only hand signals used in our planes, and they were for turns, climbs, descents, and "let go." This last was the most important. If your instructor, in the front cockpit, hit his head with his fist, you either let go of the controls or risked his turning around and beaning you! Turns were signaled when the instructor slapped an ear on the side to which the turn was to be made. Descent was ordered by a thumb pointing down from the palm; ascent was just the opposite. There was not much that could be done to change power. We were lucky on the ground to turn 1300 rpm using Pitcairn's best OX5 that featured beat up, heavy wooden props and the unfortunate single ignition. The lone spark plug per cylinder had to work or else.

To a 1929 student in his first hours of flying, the Orowing was a large, loose assembly of four great wings, a heavy center section obstructed by the engine's water radiator, several sets of flying wires x-ing across (landing wires on each wing between the struts), and a rudimentary landing gear with bicycle width tires at each end of a horizontal axis fastened with shock cord. It was a rough, noisy, windy apparatus, but it was a flying machine, not an engine with wings like today's planes. You flew it rather than just guiding an engine through the air. Added to all this it had no brakes; it had a tailskid. Caution was the byword if you experienced torque or a cross wind, or if you tried to turn on the ground from a standstill. Knowledgeable airmen would say it was an offshoot of the Jenny, crossed with a Curtiss Oriole.

As the 285 minutes of dual flying passed that June, around the 240th minute I felt I was mastering the basic problems of flying the monster. Fortunately it did not attempt to bite its master-to-be, saving that for the future. I flew the Orowing until November.

July, 1929

I had a total of 5-1/4 hours on the 2nd of July. Next day Jim said, "Get in there and take it around yourself." I was very lonely; I still remember I had the impression the rear cockpit seemed far from the prop with the front cockpit unoccupied. I can't be sure, but I probably made a better circuit and landing than ever before; I taxied back to Jim a changed man – I could fly: I could use an airplane for transport. Suddenly I was most anxious to get on with the 30 hours needed for the private pilot exam and ticket. Jim surprised me, as I thought he'd tell me to go around and practice solo. Instead he pointed out the more dual I could get in before my exam the better were my chances of success. He climbed back in, and of the 6 hours and 35 minutes flown that month, only 45 minutes were solo. It was just as well.

Two blows occurred during those 16 days flying; we were in the Pitcairn pattern (not formalized by regulation), when suddenly a stream of black smoke and oil gushed out of the right bank of the v-type engine cylinders. Jim leaned out to look, and his face, helmet and goggles were instantly painted thick black. He pulled in his head, threw up his goggles and signaled me to keep on flying and make an approach and landing. I cautiously avoided slipping (slipping and s-turns were standard methods of reducing approach distances); I looked only out of the left side of the cockpit. When we landed Jim explained the head had blown off one of the right cylinders. It was all very noisy and spectacular but I was happy to have company when it occurred.

During the last of my four solo hops that month, I had climbed to about 1000 feet on a calm and not too busy day when the engine cut out completely, though the propeller turned, just wind-milling. I did a 180 degree turn, and facing the field which was devoid of traffic, glided back in with the help of a little side slipping. This was my introduction to the Besling magneto problem (no one could predict when the single ignition magneto would fail, and few craftsmen could revive them again!). Of course I caught hell; my very first lesson had included, "Never turn back for a forced landing on takeoff, but choose the safest haven ahead, even at the risk of damage to the aircraft." Fortunately I met the legendary Parker much later, a North Philadelphia ignition expert who sustained me in future years when I flew Besling equipped OX5's.

August, 1929

The bosses were away from the law office for their sacred summer vacations. This permitted me to escape from downtown Philadelphia earlier in my Renault Torpedo, drive to Pitcairn Airport where I could sit on the turf beside my fellow students in the Class of Pitcairn '29 and observe, applaud, and criticize all the flying that was going on around the meadow in front of us. We could move south in case of showers to the Greek Restaurant within the Pitcairn fence (a building later taken over by Navy Recruiting).

One gusty afternoon with a strong northwest wind, we observed a resplendent landaulet motorcar stop in front of the hangar office. The chauffeur came over and asked us if we had seen an Army Curtiss Hawk land (we had not). He went back, opened the rear convertible, and we saw an elaborately dressed young lady take out her lorgnette and scan the skies. Not long afterward a Hawk came into view and circled noisily about the field. For reasons unknown, after a circle and buzz or two, the Hawk went off to the northwest and approached downwind. We were instantly on our feet running for the fire extinguishers to beat the first touchdown. The lady must have thought us mad. As luck would have it, the pilot nosed up so that he was left many feet in the air gesturing for assistance. We brought a ladder and out climbed a beautifully groomed Army officer complete with high tan boots, medals, and full dress uniform. His lady must have been as embarrassed as he was. From that moment, no one in our Class of '29 would ever forget to land (in those days of runwayless meadows) into the eye of the wind.

It wasn't more than a few days later that one of our classmates was practicing stalls a mile or so north of the airport when suddenly his Orowing went into a flat spin. We watched to see how he planned to recover, but our interest turned to horror when he got too low. We dashed to our cars and raced up the highway to a cornfield where dust was still rising. Walking toward us nonchalantly was Hop, the pilot. It seemed you could flat spin in with an Orowing and only damage the plane; Hop was unscathed. Of course none of us ever tried a similar feat.

The boss man at Pitcairn in '29 was Jim Ray, Harold Pitcairn's chief pilot, then a preeminent auto-gyro test pilot (who landed one on the White House lawn) and the manager of Pitcairn Airlines, flying Harold's Mailwing airplanes to Boston and Richmond. We knew and liked Jim, but he was so busy we saw little of him.

I was soloing an Orowing locally when a summer storm coaxed some cumulus clouds together northwest of the airfield. I eased off to the southeast towards Bryn Athyn to avoid the clouds, and seeing beneath me the original Pitcairn field I circled several times and landed (expertly I believed). By the time I'd turned around and started taxiing, a Pitcairn Fleetwing landed, and its lone occupant and pilot jumped out and ran toward me; it was Jim Ray. I thought I was about to be greeted and praised for my enterprise. Jim came up, reached in and shut off my engine and proceeded to read me the riot act. "When you are a student and see a storm approaching your base, you never fly away from it; you fly towards it and between it and your base if you can. Once you get away from base and the storm comes in, you are trapped." Jim and I pushed the two planes into the old hangar and sat out the storm. What a lesson! I learned that real operators like Jim have a sixth sense and will save their flock in an emergency.

September 1929

In early September I was 15 minutes shy of 16 hours, but inspectors were few in number and hard to find. One had visited Pitcairn in mid-July when I had about 9 hours, so I took both the flight and written exams and passed. Other students had arranged for a notary so the inspector could certify, but the inspector was too harried to wait until I could get back with a nearby Justice of the Peace, so I had to wait until his next visit on September 15th. He issued my certificate as of the next day, September 16th: Number 845 it was, a fair indication of the number of certified pilots in the U.S. By then I had exactly 17 hours 10 minutes.

The most exciting day was not September 16th, however, but 2 days before. I had often wondered what it would be like to land on water, since my family owned a summer home on a Maine lake. An advertisement appeared (circulated as it turned out to all student pilots who had passed a medical). Savoia-Marchetti was about to manufacture a two place biplane amphibian, the S56, in a plant they purchased on the inner tip of Port Washington's eastern peninsula. A prototype was being flown and interested parties could sign up for a demonstration. I went out to the plant, and shortly thereafter was put in the left hand seat of the S56 by the test pilot (as if I could fly it). After my first water takeoff, we flew to the East River, landed and took off, then headed for Roosevelt Field where we landed on wheels and tailskid before returning to the factory, where we circled and landed in the bay. We lowered wheels and taxied up the ramp. I'll never forget my thrill, sadly dampened days later when I read the test pilot was killed performing certification maneuvers.

October-November 1929

I only flew 3 hours 20 minutes solo and 9 hours 50 minutes

dual as days shortened and the law business increased. But two events left memories, the second a lasting result. A fellow student, Bill Page, bought a Gypsy Moth (the U.S. version built in Haverhill, Massachusetts), and took me up (duals installed). Not only did I have the privilege of sampling a delightfully light, early, flyable plane, but it had an impact starting capability, folding wings for storage, slots on the leading edge of the upper wings which would snap out as a stall approached. All this was too much for two overconfident students. A couple weeks later we staged what we then thought was a dogfight. Our inept maneuvering caught the attention of our instructors who chastised us for our antics. I was toned down by being assigned to an Orowing with a wooden rudder instead of fabric and tube. To move the rudder pedals required the strength of an ox. Even in flight they refused to budge except with the expenditure of all one's energy.

Air fields were sparse in those days; we were taught to land in farm fields as a precaution. The father of a fellow lawyer owned a farm in Feasterville, Pennsylvania, a suburb of Philadelphia. I had used it to practice landings and takeoffs. It was best to use a friend's field to avoid trespass and breach of the Regulations. The owner was a bankruptcy referee with offices on the 9th floor of our building. One autumn day he called my office and suggested I come right down with a $660 check if I wanted to buy an airplane. This, my first aircraft, purchased from the bankrupt Crescent Aviation, Inc., awaited me on a field along the west side of Roosevelt Boulevard, just north of where, later, Philadelphia's Northeast Airport was built.

My plane turned out to be most of an OX5 Kreider-Reisner

Challenger. The empenage and one of the four wings were missing, along with less critical items, including the pilot's headrest (an item I never came to own and never missed). We took all we found in a trailer to the famous barn at the south end of Pitcairn field where wrecks were being stored and gave all hands a list of missing parts. Due to the high rate of minor crackups at that time, rapid progress was achieved and my life was changed forever. From that day onward I was always the owner of at least one aircraft, even during active duty when the use of my personal planes had to be delegated while I flew combat missions.

I kept a ship's log from November 1929 to July 1935 covering my first three aircraft and a couple of loaners, and a cash account of all aircraft billings through October of 1935. I used the information for published articles, one in Western Flying for June 1936.

As for the OX5 Challenger, sleek, fast and powerful compared to the Orowings, Frank and Jim Faulkner took over when the mechanics thought it was flyable. Frank ran it up on the ground and found its prop turned at a remarkable 1380 rpm in still air on the ground. Off he went, and in level flight it turned up 1450 rpm. He flew 26 minutes, finding the aircraft "left wing and tail heavy." A little adjustment of bracing wire and it was ready for identification as NC4454. Jim flew for 35 minutes the next day just to be sure.

My first flight in the OX5 (historic to me) was to Fasmer Cox Field, across Lake Carnegie from the Princeton University Stadium, where Jim deposited my current beauty and me to attend a football game and make our way home as best we could. Next, Frank Faulkner and I flew to Ludington Airport (the site of Philadelphia International Airport today) seeking an inspector so NC4454 could be licensed. Finding no inspectors, we flew to Central Airport in Camden, New Jersey, where the ship was inspected by a representative of the Aeronautics Branch of the Department of Commerce; we filled out and signed the appropriate forms. Expeditions proudly followed, always with an instructor or engine expert: to Norristown, Coatesville, Conshohocken, Bryn Mawr, all in Pennsylvania, Hagerstown in Maryland, and Camden, New Jersey. In Hagerstown, 3 hours down, we bought a new wing from the factory (Fairchild had just bought Kreider-Reisner). The flight back (downwind) took only 1-1/4 hours; wind really affected a 70 mph aircraft! Camden had a runway, the first I ever encountered. It was asphalt with a sprinkling of cinders on top. I three-pointed fairly well but the old tail skid lived up to its name, skidding from side to side; the cinders were serving as lubricants for the skid's metal shoe. I shot a few more landings, learning to offset incipient ground loops by applying violent, prompt opposite rudder.

I had an uncle who lived on Township Line, between Elkins Park and Jenkintown, Pennsylvania. A battery and booster switch had been installed on my OX5 to fire a plug. I was taught how to prime the engine and set the prop so that I could start the engine without cranking (on boost). I flew into a hayfield near my uncle's, secured the plane and walked over to visit with him. Never was I so depressed by his complete lack of interest. He did not even walk back with me to see my plane. But wonders of wonders, I primed the OX5, set the prop, and BANG, the plane started on boost and off I went. No one was in sight or interested in the unusual presence of a plane in what was soon to become suburbia.

December 1929

This tale could go on and on, but will end at my so-called weaning, which was achieved to the satisfaction of the powers that be (or were) at Pitcairn. Word came down the line that it was not in my best interest, now that I could fly, to remain at Harold Pitcairn's comparatively expensive aviation center. There was, I was told, a remarkably able character, a flying Dutchman named Ernie Buehl, who maintained an airfield nearby in Somerton; was I to move my plane there, we would be big frogs in a small pond. I flew over, met Ernie, and settled in to a happy future with the skilled Dutchman handling my plane and its successors. I became a habitual salesman and missionary for aviation, taking friends and relatives up for hops. My flight log began to indicate the agonies of ownership, such as:

- Landing gear bending under right side
- Tail skid shock cord out
- Stabilizer adjusted
- Precautionary landing to test gas level
- Borrowed magneto, mine being fixed to prevent condensation

In this airportless era, I made a final cross-country trip to Pocono Summit with Frank Faulkner, cruising the neighborhood in search of suitable landing fields, to share my burden and debate the choices.